To China and Back

To China and Back

Anthony Bollback

Christian Publications

CAMP HILL, PENNSYLVANIA

Christian Publications
3825 Hartzdale Drive, Camp Hill, PA 17011

The mark of ✝ *vibrant faith*

ISBN: 0-87509-444-9
LOC Catalog Card Number: 90-86214
© 1991 by Christian Publications
All rights reserved
Printed in the United States of America

91 92 93 94 95   5 4 3 2 1

Cover photo illustration
© 1991, Karl Foster

Scripture taken from the HOLY BIBLE: NEW
INTERNATIONAL VERSION. Copyright © 1973, 1978,
1984 by the International Bible Society. Used by
permission of Zondervan Bible Publishers.

Dedication:

To my dear wife, Evelyn
who has given me inspiration
and encouragement through the years

and

to my four children
James, Joy, Judy and Jonathan
whose love and understanding have brought me so
much joy

I dedicate this account of our lives.

Contents

Acknowledgements

THE SEEDS FOR THIS BOOK were planted in my mind by my wife Evelyn in 1977 as we were preparing to leave Honolulu after six years of ministry in Kapahulu Bible Church of The Christian and Missionary Alliance. At that time I made a statement that she would not let me forget. "Someday I'm going to write a book about all the things that have happened to us!"

I didn't really mean it. I was simply bewildered then, as at other times in the past, by the way God was leading us. Evelyn's persistence encouraged me to write something at least for our children and grandchildren—a record of God's workings in our lives.

I am grateful for her prodding. Without that encouragement I would no doubt be still dreaming about doing it.

Words cannot begin to express my deep appreciation for Joy Peters, my daughter, who spent many hours reading and editing the manuscript as well as advising me on content. Her diligence in seeing this project through in spite of her own busy schedule has kept me at the task.

The editorial staff of Christian Publications has offered me invaluable advice and assistance in preparing this book for publication. Without that help this would merely be a record for my children.

Anthony G. Bollback
Omaha, Nebraska
January 1991

Foreword

IT IS A DISTINCT DELIGHT and honor to pen these words for my dear friend and colleague of many years in China and Hong Kong, Anthony Bollback. In this volume he has sought to magnify the Lord by sharing what God has done through him even as the Psalmist admonished: "tell of [his] wonderful works" (Psalm 26:7, KJV).

The Christian and Missionary Alliance is comprised of men and women who seek to obey God and follow the heavenly vision by demonstrating the faithfulness of Him who not only calls His people but promises that He will never leave nor forsake them. True to this heritage, Tony and Evelyn Bollback obeyed God. And, God demonstrated His faithfulness in and through their lives.

This testimony will be an encouragement to all who seek to please God in a similar manner.

Paul H. Bartel
Santa Barbara, California

1

Bishop of Coudersport

THE LETTER THAT MORNING IN JULY 1943 started Evelyn and me on an exciting journey with God. We did not know it then, but there would be wonderful surprises, bushels of joy, some disappointments and just enough heartaches for God to weave His beautiful pattern of victory and blessing into our lives.

Just weeks before, I had graduated from A.B. Simpson's Missionary Training Institute (now Nyack College) with a major in Missions. My fiancee, Evelyn Watson, who had graduated the year before, was already putting theory into practice at the Eighth Avenue Day Nursery in Newark, New Jersey. Remuneration was minimal but the provision of room and board made it an attractive place for young women to fulfill the requirements of The Christian and Missionary Alliance for home service prior to going overseas. The rigors of city life, coupled with the stern discipline of Miss Edith Morgan, the director of the nursery, soon weeded out all who maintained only a romanticized view of missions.

I am still not sure whether Edith Morgan was prepared for Evelyn's arrival! The dinner hour was customarily a somber occasion with minimal scintillating conversation—that is, until Evelyn arrived. It wasn't long until "Miss Irrepressible" had everything rolling in high gear, and fun and laughter took over. Even Edith Morgan seemed to welcome this intrusion into the tranquility of her home, for months later she not only insisted that we use the nursery facilities for our wedding reception, but she and her staff also did the decorating. In fact, until her death, Edith Morgan was a faithful prayer partner while we served in China.

I hastily tore open the envelope to see what Rev. E.C. Anderson, superintendent of the Western Pennsylvania District, had to say in reply to my application for a pastorate. Only 21 years of age, I had been entertaining visions of a beautiful church building with a sizable congregation. Surely there was some challenging place for me to begin making use of all the knowledge of homiletics and theology I'd gained at Nyack.

"I am sorry to say there are no vacant churches for you to candidate in at this time." I could hardly believe my eyes. No place to serve? Why then had he encouraged me to apply to his district when he spoke in chapel at Nyack only a few months earlier? I laid the letter down.

"Read on. Finish the letter," God seemed to say. "Maybe you've jumped to a wrong conclusion." Reading further, I came to the second surprise—no churches were open, but the district was planning to begin new churches in several towns in the northeastern sector. I could have a whole town! I could be the "Bishop of Coudersport!"

The next three days were spent in fasting and prayer, my first experience at discovering God's will in this way. During those three days, God impressed Scripture after Scripture upon my mind. Mr. Anderson had promised $25 a month subsidy for one year for the rent of a storefront meeting place. My personal needs would be God's part, he said, and if God was directing the move, then He would supply all my needs. As an afterthought he added, "Good soldiers are willing to endure hardness for Jesus' sake!"

That sounded like a challenge to me. With mounting enthusiasm and a firm conviction that God had opened a door of service to me, I did what was to become a lifelong pattern: I accepted the challenge. Flushed with excitement, I wrote Evelyn a letter and asked her to set our wedding date for August since I would start the new church in September.

An eternity passed as I waited for her response. Would she agree to go to Coudersport with no assurance of a roof over her head and no money for support? Would she give up the spartan security of the nursery for the biggest mountain we had ever dreamed of climbing?

When her reply finally arrived, it was a big "Yes." And she added, "If you know God is leading you to do this, then I will trust Him, too. I will go anywhere He leads."

We were married in the Alliance church in Newark, New Jersey on August 14, 1943. One week later, we got off the Greyhound bus at 5 p.m. in Coudersport with two suitcases, $200 and an enormous amount of confidence in the God who had called us to plant a church.

Rev. James Steele, a pastor from neighboring Emporium, was there to meet us. Standing on the corner, we could see all of Coudersport's business district—two blocks of stores in each direction. Pastor Steele led us to a vacant store and said, "I think this will make a good location for the church. It's the best available place in town. We'll come back on Monday to make rental arrangements."

As we were climbing into his car a woman approached us. Jim Steele beamed from ear to ear as he introduced us as the new pastor and wife of the Alliance church in Coudersport. "Where are you going to live?" she asked.

"We don't know yet; God hasn't told us."

The lady's eyes sparkled as she replied, "How would you like to rent my home for the next two months while I am in Florida? You can have it fully furnished for $10 a month." Would we like to! We hadn't been in Coudersport more than 30 minutes and God had already provided a home for us.

Monday we moved in.

2

Beets, Beets and More Beets

MONDAY AFTERNOON JIM STEELE AND I visited the owner of the store and signed a one-year contract for $25 a month. Brother Steele made it very clear to me that the $25 subsidy would be cut in half the second year and then be terminated.

We cleaned and painted the store and built a pulpit and altar rail. I remember well the day Jim Steele and I proudly surveyed our handiwork. "Anytime you need anything, just let me know," he offered.

"Brother Steele," I replied, "I will never tell anyone my needs except the Lord." This was a conviction I had developed through the influence of two ladies from my home church in Brooklyn, New York.

Miss Kitty Van Dyck and Miss Laura Littlefield, who lived together, had taken a special interest in my family and me. They had challenged me to read the life of Hudson Taylor and Pastor Hsi of the China Inland Mission. Their conversation often turned to China and they seemed to want to impress on me the joy of trusting God as Hudson Taylor had. The fact that Hudson Taylor never made his needs known to man made a deep impression on me, so deep, in fact, that not once in the three years we lived in Coudersport did we ever tell anyone of our financial needs.

At one point in the early days we asked the Lord to provide us with some food. A farmer by the name of Fred Postlewaite, who lived about 15 miles out of town, arrived at our door a few days later with a bushel of beets and said, "Brother Anthony, God told me you folks needed some food. I brought you this bushel of beets." We were overjoyed to see those beets. God had answered our prayers!

It wasn't many days, however, until the euphoria of answered prayer lost some of its thrill in the repetition of beets and more beets and still more beets! How many ways can you prepare beets when all you have to go with them is bread and peanut butter? And what about the beet greens? Lulu Campbell and her husband Jim had prayed that an Alliance church would be opened in Coudersport. God spoke to them also, and just about the time we were learning new and imaginative ways to prepare beets, Lulu came along with a large bag of beet greens for soup!

We decided to follow Elijah's example—he never breathed a word of complaint to anyone about the food the ravens brought. We didn't either. But a bushel of beets, even for the most spiritual, can be a trying experience, so we prayed for some variety. About the time that the bottom of the basket began to appear, God sent Fred Postlewaite to our back door again. He was grinning from ear to ear. "Brother B," he said, "God told me you folks would be needing some more food so I said to Bessie, 'I'm going into town; the Bollbacks need more food.'" Visions of delicious corn, beans and potatoes filled my mind. When the trunk lid went up, there was another bushel of beets!

"Not more beets, Lord! We asked You to supply us with food!"

Jesus gently answered, "Beets are nourishing food! I promised to supply all your needs, and right now you need beets!"

My dad had taken some vacation time to come and build a platform in the church. Although he had planned to stay a week, I soon ran out of jobs for him. After just three days he packed up and left. The real reason, however, was the beets. He had had enough to last a lifetime!

Not long after Fred Postlewaite brought the second bushel of beets, he stopped by again. I couldn't help but wonder if he had another bushel of beets for us. However, this time he reached into his pocket and pulled out $15 and with a big smile said, "I just sold a bull at the auction this morning and here is my tithe. Use it for yourselves to buy whatever you need. I always give God my tithe right away." And then with a twinkle in his eye, he added, "Do you need any more beets?"

Another time Fred stopped by with a juicy piece of venison. The deer had been in his potatoes and he got a special permit to shoot it. And, well, you have to tithe deer also, don't you? "Yes sir," said Fred. "Never cheat God of anything!"

Good old Fred! One day he brought us a squirrel he had shot. We couldn't find a recipe for squirrel, so Evelyn tried roasting it. The squirrel was so tough it finally ended up in the soup pot. Surprisingly, it was delicious. Actually almost anything would have been delicious as long as it wasn't beets.

After one year God directed me to contact Rev. Gordon Keeney of the Alliance church in Lockport, New York to come for a week of evangelistic meetings. He not only came but he brought food from the people of his church to help us entertain their pastor. This congregation continued to care for us in various ways even though we were in a different district. It was the beginning of a wonderful relationship which continued through all of our years in China and Hong Kong.

What days those were with Gordon! There weren't many people to preach to, but he kept saying to the few who came, "Wait until next year at this time. You are really going to see a big difference." He truly believed that a breakthrough would come, and he encouraged us to be patient and work hard.

At the time we were living behind the storefront church in a large 15' by 15' room. Our kitchen table was on one side, the bed next to it and the large stove across from that. In one corner there was a small sink. The bathtub was a large metal tub moved into the middle of the room when needed.

After each evening service that week, the three of us would sit on the bed with our backs against the wall as Gordon prompted us to tell him our hopes and dreams for the future. One of the things which amused him very much was the fact that I had married my pastor! Evelyn, who graduated from Nyack one year before I did, went into New York City to serve in the Greenpoint Gospel Mission. This small church had been under the leadership of Miss Cassie Van Dyck for almost 40 years. She must have been nearly 80 when she retired and only did so when the people agreed to call another woman to shepherd them. Since Evelyn and I were already engaged, my dad, among others, thought it would be a great idea if Evelyn would become their leader. The plan was that I would take over after we were married, but no one ever verbalized that. In light of Evelyn's effective ministry, the best thing I ever did was to refuse to succeed my wife as pastor!

Gordon came again the next year for another week of evangelism. This time there was a rather large crowd of people and we were all encouraged. During one of our night vigils on the bed Gordon told us about a country church near Lockport where he was holding Sunday afternoon meetings. Since the Northeastern District wanted to bring this group into the Alliance, we accepted

Gordon's invitation to speak there as a candidate.

When we saw the church, we both felt called immediately! It was a lovely white frame country chapel with a steeple and bell. It had everything I had ever dreamed of, including people. Following the morning service, the board extended a unanimous call to us right on the spot. Imagine, 40 people wanted us! At that moment we wanted them too. Buoyant with joy and thrilled with the salary offer of $35 a week, we accepted the call without ever giving a thought to seeking God's will in the matter.

Driving back to Pennsylvania on Monday, we were filled with plans and dreams. Approaching Coudersport, however, the excitement began to subside and the last miles into town became clouded with a heaviness like the stillness before an approaching storm. Why the gloom, we wondered? More than a year of effort had been put into this new church and there was very little to show for it. We had given it our best. We deserved a change and most of all we deserved this great opportunity of a larger ministry. We deserved people! Surely no one would question the rightness of that.

We parked the 1929 Chevrolet in its spot by the back door, entered our one windowless room and set our bags down. We looked around our home and then at each other. "We've made a mistake. We didn't talk to God about this move. He is not finished with us in Coudersport."

The only telephone available was at the corner

drug store. My heart was beating wildly as I dialed Gordon Keeney to tell him we would not be coming after all. Gordon was truly a man of God with great spiritual discernment. He understood what God was doing in our lives and encouraged us to be faithful no matter what others might think. The district superintendent was not as understanding. His letter informed me that I would never serve another church in his district as long as he was superintendent. I was undependable, he said.

Despite the times when we felt weighed down with problems, God continued to supply our needs. We had purchased a 1929 Chevy for the astronomical sum of $75. It lacked many things, including good tires.

One night we were driving to a nearby town to provide special music and preach at the Alliance church, when suddenly, I realized the right tire was flat. As I got out to survey the damage, one of the ladies who had come with us said, "Pastor, you've got two flats!" Sure enough, both right tires were flat! Changing the first tire was no problem. It was the second one that was not so easy, for in those days tires had inner tubes that had to be patched.

Repairs made, we were soon cruising along at 35 miles an hour. We arrived at the church in high spirits just as the two left tires went flat! I couldn't believe that on one night, within 50 miles of home, anyone could have four flat tires! When I explained to the congregation why we were almost late a man in the church got up out of his seat, went to his garage and replaced the four inner tubes with good ones he had just taken out of his own car. We drove that car without ever having another flat and then finally sold it for $95!

One day John and his wife Vivian, from the nearby Alliance church in Harrison Valley, stopped by to see how we were and to inquire if we needed anything. We assured them that we were doing just fine and that the Lord was providing all of our needs. The fact was that we had hardly anything left for our Sunday meals.

On their way home, the Lord spoke to John and said, "The Bollbacks don't have any food for Sunday. Go and buy them some groceries." "But," John reasoned with the Lord, "if that were the case, they would have told us." However, a persistent voice urged him to turn around. This time he reasoned that he didn't want to make a fool of himself or insult us. And so he drove on until the third call came to him from the Lord.

About an hour after he had left, John appeared at our door with two armloads of groceries and scoldingly said, "Why didn't you tell us you didn't have any food in the house? You would have saved me a lot of extra driving," and then added laughingly, "but I should have listened to God the first time."

Coudersport was God's school of obedience for us. Although we didn't realize it then, the lessons learned there would be invaluable in the days ahead.

3

God Moves In

THE DECISION TO STAY in Coudersport seemed to open heaven's windows, and blessings began to be poured out on us. Almost overnight people started attending the church.

Andy and Beryl Uhlman, with their four young daughters, moved into town. Andy, who was the night foreman at the hosiery mill, began introducing his Christian friends to the boss. It was through his influence that Herb Greenwood moved from North Carolina to become manager of the plant. Within weeks these two solid Christian families began attending the church. The Greenwoods' three children added to our growing Sunday school, and Herb became the first Sunday school superintendent.

Walt Goodman, a bachelor friend of Andy Uhlman, was just what we needed to cement the Campbell family to us. Their two daughters, Thelma and Marge, in their 20s, were talented singers and leaders at the local Free Methodist church. Thelma was already married to an Alliance man who was serving overseas in the army. And before long, I performed my first wedding ceremony by uniting Walt and Marge. Soon the congregation was topping 40—more people than in the pretty country church near Lockport. Week by week the attendance grew, along with the anticipation of great things to come.

Sensing a need for an evangelistic outreach in the town, I invited Rev. Sam McGarvey, a classmate from Nyack, to come and preach for two weeks. Nothing special happened the first week. But on Sunday, following the morning message, the congregation gathered at the altar to pray. We prayed for the salvation of people, for the quickening of Christians and for the onward movement of God in this young church. People forgot the hour as prayer continued long into the afternoon. That night God answered our prayers.

Mrs. Furman, a godly woman who became like a mother to us, received a great blessing in the morning service. She went home and began calling all of her friends on the party line. The news of the morning service spread rapidly, for even those she didn't call were listening in! That night, among others, Mr. and Mrs. Wade and their four children were present. Again, the power of God was so real and the preaching so powerful that at the invitation they rushed to the altar and prayed with tears to receive Christ into their lives.

Rarely have I seen new Christians change so radically and so quickly. Mr. Wade wasted no time telling everyone what had happened to him. The result was similar to the times Jesus performed His miracles—the crowds came to see what was happening.

Monday morning the telephone line was busy again. Between Mrs. Furman and the Wades, the whole area of Sweden Hill was moved toward God. The word got out that Mr. Wade would drive his truck down the hill and anyone who needed a ride could hop on if they didn't mind standing! What a sight it was on Main Street, Coudersport, when the truck pulled up at the church and 25 people jumped off the back end. Night after night, traffic was held up for the unloading. Nothing like this had ever happened in Coudersport.

That week about 25 people received Christ into their lives. The Alliance church in Coudersport was established. Within a few months everyone in the area had heard about the little storefront chapel, and almost 100 people were attending the services. The need for new facilities drove us once more to our knees in prayer. Again God answered.

One day Andy Uhlman stopped to tell me that a lady had offered to sell us a piece of land just off Main Street in the center of town. When the congregation heard about it, the money began to pour in. We soon had enough to purchase the property. That news reached the front page of the local paper.

The beginning of excavation was a very exciting day for all of us, but there were funds enough only for the initial payment. The balance was due in 29 days. How the people prayed and worked and sacrificed! On day 29, as I walked into the contractor's office with the full balance in hand, the burly steam shovel operator looked at me and said, "Reverend, I never expected to get paid! How did you do it?"

We were still living in the windowless room behind the church as we expected our first child. With only three months to the due date, we prayed for a new home. Unexpectedly, an apartment over the gas company office a few blocks away opened up. Now we had windows and fresh air.

About that time I was invited to hold a week of evangelistic meetings up on Sweden Hill. Mrs. Furman and her friends were all firmly planted in our church in town, but they were concerned for neighbors who would not drive that far for services. The Claus Indian Family provided the music, and I did the preaching. Many people were saved and became a part of our growing church.

God had another surprise in store for us. The Clauses had purchased a house on a hill just outside of town. They asked if we would like to move in and take care of it for them. It was another wonderful provision of the Lord.

Earlier we had been ready to quit and move on. But now, a year and a half later, God was calling us to China, and our hearts were torn by thoughts of separation from those dear people, among them six young people who would enter the ministry as a result of our time there. The friendships and memories we had built in Coudersport would last a lifetime.

4

The Commitment

THERE WASN'T TIME TO MISS COUDERSPORT because each day was filled with packing and
more packing. And besides, we were beginning to see the fulfillment of a dream of many
years—a lifetime of missionary service in China.
My dad worked for the Borden Milk Company.
Their powdered milk was called Klim—milk
spelled backwards. Several cases were packed in
our barrels and labeled "special"—enough for
our infant son Jim and one or two others who
might arrive in the next seven years. The Shanghai customs, months later, had a difficult time
believing all that food was not for sale and that it
could really last seven years! And anyway, why
would anyone bring so much milk for unborn
babies? Didn't I have a wife who would nurse
the babies? And with plenty of Chinese women
around to nurse our babies if necessary, why
would anyone bring all that milk? Unbeknownst
both to them and to us, God was preparing for an
emergency three years later when two missionary
families would be forced to evacuate China.
We visited The Christian and Missionary Alliance headquarters in New York City where Dr.

A.B. Simpson had built the Gospel Tabernacle. It was customary for Dr. A.C. Snead, foreign secretary, to gather members of the Foreign Department together for a brief service of dedication. Rev. Howard Van Dyck, Dr. Snead's assistant, an honored missionary statesman from Central China, was also present that day to help commission the first new missionaries to be sent to Central China in 15 years. Rev. Van Dyck was the nephew of Miss Cassie Van Dyck, the leader of the Greenpoint Gospel Mission who had so influenced me toward China.

Dr. Snead and Mr. Van Dyck placed their hands on us as we knelt in the center of a circle of men and women from the department. In his soft, yet deeply moving voice, Dr. Snead committed us to China. It was a commitment that would take us to China and back again.

The seven years that would comprise our first term seemed like an eternity as we said goodbye to our families. But we knew we were in the center of God's will, and that was all that mattered.

With the De Soto packed to the roof and just enough room for Jim to have a comfortable bed in the back seat, we headed for the West Coast. Blinking back tears on that September morning, we were convinced that no matter what happened—even if it meant a martyr's death—there could be no turning back.

The story of John and Betty Stam of the China Inland Mission who were cruelly beheaded in 1934 at the hands of the communists was very fresh in our minds. The Van Dycks had prepared us well for any eventuality, but instead of frightening us, it spurred us forward to fill the gap. Martyrdom was no remote possibility, for in 1946 the communists were more active in China than 20 years before when the Stams had been murdered. Even optimistically, the prediction was that it would be only 10 years before all of Asia would be overrun by the communists. In spite of this, many Alliance young people were applying for missionary service in those targeted lands. There was little thought of comfort and ease—only the urgency to get the gospel to the ends of the earth while time remained.

We arrived in San Francisco 12 days later to find that a longshoremen's strike had been called. The next six weeks in California were both fascinating and frustrating, to say the least, as four missionary families lived in one four-bedroom apartment. Besides ourselves, there was Esther Kowles and her two children (Ray was already in China), George and Martha (Kowles) Tubbs with their baby and Etta Whitney. Living in such close quarters, we soon found out that missionary "halos" can get tarnished very quickly. We also discovered that halos can be polished by confession and loving understanding. It was a lesson worth learning.

5

Next Stop—China

ON DECEMBER 15, 1946 we boarded the *Marine Lynx* in San Francisco harbor for the two-week trip to Shanghai. This ship would go down in history not merely for carrying troops to the war zone, but for transporting over 700 missionaries to the Orient in the largest mass movement of missionaries on one ship in history. It was billed by the American President Lines as a "converted" troop transport. A great crowd of people gathered on the pier to witness this historic event. Paper streamers connected us to many new Alliance friends from the Bay area churches. As the ship's whistle let forth a throaty blast, the longshoremen lifted the ropes that held us captive to the pier. Slowly the ship inched away, the ropes still clinging as if reluctant to let go.

The streamers, too, became taut, grasped by our friends on the other end. Then, one by one, they snapped and the last ties with our homeland were broken. We turned and looked westward—to China.

Since this was the first civilian voyage of the *Marine Lynx* since the war the accommodations were less than desirable. The few available private cabins were reserved for government or corporate VIPs. The missionaries would bunk in the hold of the ship just as the soldiers had done. The only concession was that the bunks were just two high instead of the usual four for the troops. That was the extent of the conversion.

The men were assigned to the small holds— about 50 men to a section. My wife Evie and Jimmy were assigned to one of the large holds with 250 other women and children under six. Husbands were not allowed in the area.

The Alliance women wanted to stay together, but independent Evie had other plans. She found a bunk right next to the rest rooms. It didn't look too good to me, but she reasoned that with a one-year-old, she wanted to be close to the facilities. It proved to be an ideal spot since the rest of the hold was jammed with screaming kids, smelly diapers and sick mothers. I set up a collapsible bed for Jimmy and roped it to some pipes to keep it from sliding around in rough seas. He felt right at home in his little bunk, and Evie made the trip with no seasickness. As it turned out, everywhere else there was bedlam.

The first night, with a calm sea, we gratefully settled into our bunks. About 2 a.m., however, I was awakened by the rolling and pitching of the ship. The noises and creaks sent shivers through my heart. The crash of the waves against the bow was deafening. Each time the ship rose on a wave, it would suspend in midair for an eternal minute and then suddenly plunge down so deep that it seemed it would never rise again. I climbed out of my bunk with great difficulty only to find cold water swishing around under the bunks. My main job now was to get the dripping suitcases secured in an empty bunk and then try to keep myself from rolling out of bed. Although most of the passengers never made it to breakfast, Jack Shepherd and Bill Kerr, classmates from Nyack, and I did. There was no sign of any of the women.

Christmas Day dawned like all others on board ship. By this time, most everyone had their sea legs, and the Alliance missionaries decided to have a celebration together in one of the empty bow sections. The group included the Bartels, Pattersons, Kowles, Tubbs, Shepherds, Kerrs, Notsons, Mrs. Bressler, and Misses Oppelt, Turley, Whitney and Cuthbertson. Everyone enjoyed exchanging the small gifts we had brought especially for the occasion.

A few days later we sailed peacefully into the China Sea in brilliant sunshine. We dropped anchor the next morning and picked up the pilot, who would guide the ship into Shanghai harbor. With last-minute preparations for disembarking completed, we waited impatiently for morning to come so we could set foot on Chinese soil.

At last it came our turn to walk down the gangplank. I remembered all the Chinese tea I had drunk in the little Chinese laundry where I used to go to help a lad with his English lessons. That had been another of Kitty Van Dyck's ideas to get me interested in China. Apparently it had worked, because here I was.

The Alliance Christians of Shanghai were on hand to welcome us all—old friends and newcomers alike. Preparations had been made to put us up in a worker's home. We were warned that it would be almost bare of furniture because the Japanese had stripped everything from the place during the occupation. But the thought of even a roof over our heads was more than we expected.

A couple of hours passed while we waited our turn to board the U.S. army trucks that would take us to our destination. Finally about 6 p.m. the truck arrived, and baggage and people were loaded on. With a lurch we were off into the darkness of the Shanghai night. Two hours later, in the midst of crying babies and restless adults, our American drivers were still vainly trying to find the place. Finally, through the expert Chinese of Paul Bartel, we pulled into a very narrow street and were graciously greeted by our hosts.

Because there were so many of us, the women and children were housed in one building and the men in another. We had expected two weeks of that on board ship, but not here in Shanghai. When we got to the rooms, there was nothing in them but steel cots with Japanese floor mats for mattresses. We spread our blankets on them and were grateful to whomever had had the foresight to instruct us to bring bedding. The night was December 31, 1946. We were in China.

6

Shanghai: City of Surprises

I AWOKE WHILE IT WAS STILL DARK feeling stiff and chilled all over, my voice deep and husky from a cold that had settled in during the night. The sounds of the awakening city were to become familar over the years, but on January 1, 1947 they were all strange and intriguing.

The other missionaries were stirring, too, with the strange sounds and unaccustomed surroundings. After I greeted Jack Shepherd in a raspy voice, he said, "Oh Tony, you're sick. I hope you're not going to be our first martyr!"

We all gathered for breakfast in a lower room where the Chinese hosts did the best they could under the circumstances. We had boiling tea, peanuts and plain dry toasted bread.

Having given up getting warm with the smoky Japanese stoves provided in each room, we decided to go outdoors for a walk in the sunshine. Even in the chilling January cold of Shanghai, the sunshine seemed inviting, as did the city itself. We saw a large parade of young people beating drums, singing and shouting slogans. Attracted by the sounds and the excitement, we rushed toward the procession. Although the posters and banners didn't mean much to any of us since none of us could read Chinese yet, we appreciated the young people's vitality. One of the older missionaries found us watching the parade and quickly herded us back to our cold quarters. Safely away from the crowd, she explained that this had been an anti-American demonstration calling on the Yankees to go home!

At the New York headquarters during our indoctrination period, we had been taught that junior missionaries were subject to the authority of the senior missionaries in everything. Although an unbreakable rule, it was a difficult concept to accept, especially for the men who were all ordained pastors with several years of experience. We vowed that when we became senior missionaries, we would never be unreasonable nor would we find ourselves among the rebellious who generally didn't return to the field.

We had been asked before leaving the States to deliver a package to a Miss Edna Johnson of the Door of Hope Mission in Shanghai. A popular form of transportation in Shanghai at that time was the peddycab—a three-wheeled bicycle with a driver who pedaled from the forward position and carried two passengers behind. The peddycab trip out to the Door of Hope Mission was fascinating. Jimmy was a great attraction all along the way, and he took full advantage of those moments of popularity. This mission specialized in providing a home for girls who were discarded by families disappointed at having too many daughters. More than a hundred girls of all ages were being cared for by the missionaries and their helpers.

One of our new friends at the mission gave the peddycab driver the instructions to take us back home. Whether he misunderstood or whether the place was really that difficult to find, we will never know. But after riding around for about an hour, the driver turned to us and made it known by sign language that he didn't know where he was going. He stopped and asked several people and then started pedaling again. He stopped a second time and with an imploring look in his eyes vainly tried to get directions from us. We knew we were in big trouble.

We motioned the driver forward with the hope that we would recognize something or someone. Engulfed in a mass of swirling humanity, our only option was prayer. As we finished praying together, I opened my eyes, and there, among those hundreds of faces pushing along that crowded street, we recognized the pastor of the church we had attended on Sunday. I grabbed the driver's shirt and motioned for him to stop. Fortunately Pastor Wong was able to speak a little English, and after explaining our situation to him, we were soon on our way home.

Through the Bartels, Jack Shepherd, Bill Kerr and I were invited to the palatial home of a wealthy businessman by the name of K.S. Lee, who was prominent in the Shanghai church. Our eyes bulged, amazed at the lavish antique Oriental furniture and priceless pieces of art which he had managed to hide from the Japanese several years before. What really struck us, however, was the extreme poverty surrounding his home. Like an oasis in a parched desert, this elegant home sat amid hovels and beggars, remnants of a terrible war. It was a paradox we were never able to comprehend.

Day after day we missionary men hovered around the customs house either watching our papers being stamped or knowing that they were in a pile and could probably have reached the top in no time at all for a price. We chose to wait it out. About that time we found The Chocolate Shop, an ordinary restaurant by North American standards, but for tired, cold missionaries, it became a luxury hangout—one of the few places where there was heat. We discovered we could make a pot of hot chocolate last for about 45 minutes, and by ordering a second pot, we could stay warm for an hour and a half!

The Bartels were assigned as our senior missionary couple. Because of their loving and considerate ways, we chose to make them our models. Their lives exemplified excellence in language, a deep commitment to God and a burning passion to reach China. The Bartels decided that some of us should move on up the river about 600 miles to Wuchang. It would be more comfortable for the women and children, they said, and much less expensive than Shanghai.

Miss Oppelt was assigned as hostess of the home in Wuchang. Although she had agreed to the transfer from the South China field, her heart was never in the duties of the home, preferring to devote her time to the Chinese people rather than concerning herself with menus for language students. About the only bright spot for Miss Oppelt in her new assignment was Jimmy, who delighted in being spoiled by this doting auntie.

Bill Kerr escorted the women and children on the long trip inland, while Jack Shepherd remained behind with me to work on the freight. My job was to get the baggage released. Since Jack and I were the only young people left, we moved in together in a very cold, miserable, dirty rooming house. The Chocolate Shop became our headquarters by day, and our sleeping bags became home by night.

7

Wuchang

EVIE WAS THE FIRST TO ARRIVE in Wuchang since she was in the lead party headed by Margaret Oppelt. The main port of this tri-city area known as Wuhan was Hankou. Lying on the north bank of the river opposite Wuchang, it could be reached only by ferry. Evie was in for some unusual surprises in Hankou as the ship prepared to dock. It was the eve of Chinese New Year, the most important holiday on the Chinese calendar. Everything in China stops for three days of celebration while the people enjoy their families, fulfill their obligations to the spirits of the ancestors and watch the paper dragons parading through the streets.

At the dock there was total confusion, shouting, unbelievable noise and jostling by the rickshaw pullers, who were all vying for the "rich" foreigners to ride in their rickshaws. Besides carrying Jimmy down the gangplank in her arms, Evelyn had her trombone. The rickshaw pullers were shouting and grabbing at Jimmy to get him out of Evie's arms and into their rickshaws knowing that she would follow. Grasping Jimmy tighter than ever, she used her trombone as a bayonet

and fought off the shouting drivers until missionary Roy Birkey came to her rescue. Mr. Birkey was
the brother of Ina Bartel and the only Alliance
missionary in Central China at that time. He had
volunteered to go ahead to get the missionary
home repaired and ready for occupancy, leaving
his wife Betty behind to follow as soon as possible. The Japanese had vacated the building
after using it for years as their headquarters in
Wuchang. They had actually stabled their horses
in the basement area of this huge home.

Finally the party was able to make its way to the
Lutheran Home in Hankou to spend the next few
days until the holiday was over and they could
cross the river. Rev. and Mrs. Arthur Hansen,
Alliance missionaries, operated the home for the
Lutherans. Their service was symbolic of the
strong ties between our missions. Alliance children also attended the Lutheran school at Jigong
Shan (Rooster Mountain) in Hunan Province,
where our missionaries spent their summers to
escape the extreme heat of the plains.

Meanwhile, I was down in Shanghai camping
out at The Chocolate Shop and waiting impatiently for my turn to go up river. The day finally
arrived when our customs papers were cleared
and our things were loaded on the river steamer
for the 600-mile trip. Along the way I visited the
city of Wuhu, where Howard Van Dyck had lived
for so many years. As I walked through the
streets, my mind was filled with images of the
little church in Greenpoint and the red silk ban-

ners that had prompted my first interest in this mysterious land. My heart overflowed with joy as I realized how God had worked in my life to bring me to this spot. I had obeyed His directions and had followed His call. At that moment there wasn't anything I wanted to do more than just follow Him anywhere in China, or the world, for that matter.

By the end of February, our barrels were safely stored in the basement of the big mission house. The next step was unpacking, getting settled and starting language school. We were assigned one room on the second floor, and our meals were eaten with the other language students in the communal dining room. With the arrival of the next shipload of missionaries, the home was filled, 17 of us in all.

The Bartels had their own apartment. Jimmy was the only child among 17 language students, and since none of them had any children, they all became experts at child discipline. "Auntie" Oppelt generally gave in to Jimmy's every whim. If he wanted three dishes of pudding, "poor little Jimmy" could have them. If the "amah" (Chinese for baby sitter or helper) couldn't handle him while we were at language school, Auntie Oppelt would entertain him by giving him a big round tin of buttons. Never have I seen so many buttons in one place and neither had I seen so many scattered all over the floor by a child allowed to do as he pleased. "No problem," Miss Oppelt would say, "the amah will pick them up!"

The Wuchang home was situated on the top of a hill with a narrow alley winding its way up between the houses that had managed to escape the Japanese bombings. There was rubble everywhere, but one wall stood straight and tall amid the destruction. It bore one large Chinese character—the character for "blessing." It is also the first character used for the gospel. This wall became a silent witness to the power of God's good news.

The stone steps leading up to the big house were uneven and rough. Near the top, the road dropped off steeply to the rubble below. A high wall enclosed the property with a watchman's gatehouse at the entrance way. A small path ran alongside the wall that led to the School for the Blind where Mrs. Martin Ekvall, an elderly Alliance saint, ministered to blind girls and women. It was precarious to walk along that path with its steep dropoff, and we worried about Mrs. Ekvall making her daily trips to the school. She assured us that she was surefooted even at 80 and that this was nothing compared to the 11 wars she had already survived in China.

That precarious path, however, was soon to send shivers of fear through Evelyn and me. We had started language school at the Central China University, an Anglican school, which was located about a 20-minute walk from our house. Ah Chun was hired to be the amah to watch Jimmy. Meeting Ah Chun for the first time was a real shock. Her feet were about four inches long and when she walked, it was as if she were walking on stilts. Chinese women during their childhood had their feet bound in order to meet the beauty customs of their society.

One day as we returned home, we found Ah Chun carrying Jimmy and walking outside the wall along the precarious cliff. It looked as if she could tumble down the steep side at any moment. Jimmy was bouncing excitedly in her arms and waving at us as we climbed up the narrow path. She never understood our fears since she had been tottering around for years on her little stubby feet and besides, she reasoned, a boy should be granted "whatever he wished." Suddenly we were confronted by a conflict of cultures which drove us to daily prayer. No one had warned us that there would be so many challenges to test our commitment. The glamor of missionary life was fast disappearing.

We managed to get through the first semester and to come out with the highest test scores of the 50 students in the school. It wasn't easy for me. My mind demanded an explanation for everything. Evelyn found it easy to pick up words and phrases because she is good at mimicking. This caused me so much frustration that on one occasion I asked the Lord why He ever sent us to China. God was asking me to climb a very big mountain. With His help, I did it.

Our meals were prepared by a Chinese cook under the supervision of Miss Oppelt who, as I already mentioned, preferred "real missionary work'' with the Chinese students to kitchen duty. The menu was as predictable as the rising sun. At noon we gathered for the best meal of the day—an original one. When we arrived for the evening meal, we discovered all the leftovers from noon warmed over as a casserole. What bothered us most were the omelets that were served for breakfast. Anything left over from the casserole appeared in the omelet! One night we all ganged up on dear Miss Oppelt and brought our own food to the table. She let us know in no uncertain terms what she thought of this new breed of missionaries and how little we would ever accomplish for God. After that, however, the meals did improve.

I'll never forget the day came when the inevitable happened. Jimmy was missing! Consternation filled all of our hearts because there were so many dangerous places, including an open well amid the rubble. We searched every nook and cranny, but no Jimmy. Frantically we ran from place to place. In my excitement to find him, I had overlooked him. I had opened only one door of a double clothes closet, which was standing on the veranda. Some time later, Evelyn opened both doors and there, crouching in a corner sucking his thumb, was our little boy.

There was one rule of the Wuchang home that we all enjoyed very much. Roy Birkey decreed that at 4 p.m. everyone must quit studying until after the evening meal and get out to play volleyball or take a walk on Snake Hill near the home.

All work and no play, he believed, made missionaries dull people!

If the old Wuchang house could speak, what stories it would tell, like the night that Joe Vandergrift and I decided to rent some bikes and go buy some Chinese almond cakes while our wives made hot chocolate at home.

On the way to the store Joe's bike hit a large hole in the concrete street. The jolt broke the frame of the decrepit bike at the main section of the front wheel. Joe flew headfirst to the ground and lay there unconscious.

I managed to get him into a rickshaw, loaded the broken bike in a second rickshaw and headed for home. On the way, we stopped at the bike shop. They wanted me to pay for repairs! My Chinese wasn't too good, but it was good enough to let them know I had no intention of paying for anything.

The sight of Joe, by now conscious but somewhat dazed and bleeding, coupled with my threats of terrible things to come if he died because of their old junk, convinced them to settle the whole matter without further demands.

Our adventures, however, were not nearly over. Joe needed medication. So another missionary and I got our flashlights and headed to the hospital. It was after 10 p.m. and no one was supposed to be on the streets because of the curfew. We started through the long Snake Hill tunnel, which was heavily guarded by soldiers because of the fear of communist guerrillas blowing it up

and dividing the city. Suddenly out of the darkness came the order to halt. We shone the flashlights on ourselves to let the guards see that we
were foreigners and unarmed. After explaining
why we were out, they allowed us to pass.

And about the hot chocolate and almond
cakes?

Well, some lucky Chinese probably picked up
the bag of almond cakes off the street. And hours
later, as we watched over Joe (who had suffered a
slight concussion), we sipped the hot chocolate
and recounted the excitement of the evening.

8

Rooster Mountain

SUMMERS IN THE YANGZI RIVER VALLEY are very hot and oppressive. The nights can best be described as one long sauna under a mosquito net with a million insects intoning an incessant lullaby. We have fallen asleep on many a torrid night to the hum of a mosquito orchestra frantically attempting to reach the humans inside.

It was announced that the language students would all be moving to the higher elevation at Jigong (pronounced Gee Gung) for three months. It was welcome news. At Rooster Mountain we would enjoy cooler weather and fewer mosquitos. We would also see the Lutheran missionary school and home where the Alliance missionaries of Central China had sent their children for many years. We expected that one day our children would attend there as well.

Paul Bartel, with his usual concern for the comfort of the young missionaries under his care, announced that June and July would be a continuation of our language study, and August would be a much-needed vacation break from the rigors of seven months of concentrated work. We packed our bags with enthusiasm. Before the Sino-Japanese war, Jigong had been a delightful place with many western-style summer homes owned by various missions or individuals. But with the outbreak of the war, these homes had been left to the mercy of the local residents, who stripped them of anything they could carry away.

We, along with the Vandergrifts, decided to take over Sunset Cottage which belonged to some retired Alliance missionaries. There was lots to be done to make the place livable. We took cots, sleeping bags, the bare essentials for cooking, and of course, our trusted young cook who came from Jigong. Little did we know that within a few months his presence would prove to be God's wonderful provision for our evacuation needs.

August brought a lot of rumors about the movement of the communist brigades that were pressuring Hankou and Wuchang (where we had been living), the industrial center for Central China. Some brigades had even penetrated the city at night, causing alarm and fear among the city residents and anxiety among the missionaries. Now a "reliable" report began circulating that the communists were intending to break through to Chi Kung Shan (where we now were) and blow up the train tunnel, thus isolating 150 or more foreigners on the mountain top. That would be a significant bargaining chip in their struggle for power. I was approaching my 25th birthday and Evelyn was planning a celebration. The party, however, turned out differently than any of us expected.

The Lutheran missionaries who were responsible for this area kept in close touch with their Chinese friends. The reports were becoming more alarming by the day. On the night of August 27, 1947, we were still savoring the flavor of a delicious chocolate birthday cake when all of the men were hurriedly summoned to the chapel to hear the reports and consider evacuation. The decision was made to leave the next morning. There would be one train departing about 10 a.m. Everyone was urged to be on it.

What we didn't realize that night was that a few hundred other people had the same idea! Near the missionary colony stood a large hotel where business people congregated. They rarely associated with the "religious fanatics" on the other ridge, but each knew of the existence of the other group and in times of crisis helped each other. Some U.S. government people there who had a link with Washington kept us informed of emergencies.

Evie and Mary Vandergrift were waiting for Gillette and me to return. At 11 p.m. we rushed in with the news. We finished off the birthday cake and feverishly began to pack our few belongings. The house had to be closed up for any eventuality and since Vandergrifts had no children, they decided to postpone their departure a few days. We all worked through the night and caught only a few winks of sleep.

Not being as wise as the senior missionaries who had evacuated on several other occasions during their years in China, we waited until morning to send our cook into the little village to find some men and a sedan chair for Evie, who was pregnant at the time. As we were finishing our packing, he returned with the news that all of the carriers had already started down the mountain. Not one was available. And to make matters worse, the train would be leaving before the carriers could make it back up to take us down.

Evacuations were new to us, but calling on the Lord was not, so we prayed and committed ourselves to the Lord. Then, taking whatever we could carry, we started walking down the mountain. The Vandergrifts planned to bring the main baggage later with their things, but there were three valuable things we chose to take with us: Jimmy (of course), Evelyn's trombone and my violin.

Evelyn was responsible to keep Jimmy walking along as fast as possible. I had the instruments and a suitcase, and the cook had our personal effects slung across his shoulders carrier-style.

The path took us through a little village at the top of the mountain. What a comical sight we must have been trudging along, carrying our own baggage. Foreigners never did that in China. Entering the center of the village, we saw some grannies squatting over wash boards chatting excitedly, no doubt, about the financial woes of the village now that the foreigners were all leaving so suddenly. As we came into view, the women stopped their conversations, jumped up and surrounded us. Jimmy got his full share of cheek pinching as they asked our cook what we were doing. One of the grannies began to bark orders. In China, when the matriarch speaks, everyone listens. Before we knew what was happening, several men gathered around. A large vegetable basket was emptied, and Jimmy was placed in it.

Soon a dusty sedan chair was brought out and placed on the ground and the granny motioned Evie into the chair. Everyone was obeying her commands without questioning, and so did we. The granny now ordered some reluctant young men to carry Evie down the hill. With Jimmy seated comfortably in the vegetable basket and our bags suspended on the other end of the bamboo pole, a young man raised it to his shoulder and carried it down the hill. For Jimmy it was a chariot fit for a king. God had answered our prayers in a most miraculous way.

About halfway down the mountain we got our first glimpse of the train station. The train was already there, belching black smoke. Surrounding the train was a mass of people, like ants scurrying this way and that, all intent on somehow getting on board. Once more, the situation seemed hopeless. Even if we did get down the mountain in time, could we get on the train?

Down at the station, we paid the carriers generously for the extra trouble and found ourselves in the midst of the mass of frantically pushing, shoving, shouting people. One look at the train gave us a clear message—there was absolutely no

chance that we would get on. People were already
perched on the roof of the simple wooden box
cars, which had rows of benches without backs
and windows cut in the sides.

We inched our way down the platform searching for some way to get on board. Just then a
German missionary doctor we had met up on the
hill saw us in the crowd and called out that we
should go to the end of the train. There was no
time for an explanation. We simply pushed forward, believing that God was giving us more directions. It looked just as hopeless at the end of
the train, but then we noticed a little space on the
outside platform of the last car. The conductor
was preventing others from boarding the platform, but he graciously made way for us, helping
Evie up the steps. We sighed with relief. We were
on board. God had intervened and sent an angel
in the form of a friendly conductor.

The departure was long overdue, but that was
normal for Chinese trains. Often a train had to
stop for an hour or so just to get up enough steam
to make the mountain ahead. There was no telling when this one would leave, but at least we
were on board. About that time, an engine pushing a car with glass windows slowly approached
the train. The conductor waved it forward until,
with a clang and a lurching jolt, it was coupled to
us. We were surprised at the elegance of the car.
Imagine—glass windows and compartments. For
that part of China and for those times, it was

really first-class. We discovered it was a private car for the wealthy guests from the hotel.

Because of the obvious contrast between this car and the rest of the train, the mob didn't attempt to board. The gap between China's wealthy few and her poor masses had never been breached, a situation that helped to provide fertile ground for the communists to later incite the populace against the rich. The terrible excesses of the cultural revolution in the '60s, when peasants became lords of the rich, was a prime example of the existing sentiments.

With the special car attached, the train was ready to leave. A blast of the whistle warned everyone to hang on tight for the lurch that always accompanied the startup of the train. It picked up speed quite quickly without seeming regard for those still trying to clamber aboard.

Our first task was to get as comfortable on our suitcases as possible. There was a long trip ahead of us with no food and no comfort facilities. However, a few minutes before as the special hotel car was being coupled to the train, the manager of the hotel recognized us. We had been to the hotel a few nights previous for a gathering of the language students and had all been introduced to him. After greeting us warmly, he disappeared into the special car. He soon reappeared, and with a broad smile on his face, invited us to come into his car. He explained that there were two Russian ladies with three children in a compartment and if we didn't mind being a little crowded, they wanted to invite us to join them. The girls made a big fuss over Jimmy while the mothers did all they could to make Evelyn comfortable. This was more than we could ask or even think—sitting on leather-cushioned seats and about to enjoy a sumptuous chicken dinner prepared by the hotel.

Again, the Lord had provided for our needs.

9

Our China Doll

L ANGUAGE STUDY BACK IN WUCHANG continued at a different pace for Evelyn after the
summer. We had obtained permission from
our sympathetic chairman, Paul Bartel, to move
into a little apartment of our own in the big
house. We were also very fortunate that our Jigong
cook wanted to join us after the summer. The
experiences up on Rooster Mountain had made
him a real part of our family. Evelyn was granted
permission to study at home with her favorite
teacher, Mrs. Woo. Both of them embraced the
challenge the chairman had given—keep up with
the students at school. There was no problem for
these two determined women—it was the rest of
us at the language school who were desperately
trying to keep up the torrid pace they set. Evelyn
was determined to complete her work before the
baby was born. And she did.

Dr. Logan Roots and his staff of midwives were
excited about having an American baby born at
their hospital. We lived on the east side of Snake
Mountain, which bisected the city from north to
south. The hospital could only be reached by
passing through a long tunnel. From the house to

47

the hospital was about two miles, but it seemed like 10,000 for Evelyn in a bumpy rickshaw.

Joy was born on February 17, 1948. I was allowed in the delivery room provided I stayed out of the way. The elderly midwife, who supervised the delivery under the watchful eyes of Dr. Roots, picked Joy up a few moments after birth and held her up like Anna of the New Testament must have held Jesus. She then prayed in Chinese a prayer of praise and dedication. Nothing could have been more beautiful.

The doctor's wife, Mamie, was watching out for Evelyn, but it was a Chinese hospital and Chinese customs prevailed—two weeks bed rest and an additional two in seclusion. The midwife was on hand to see that Evelyn obeyed. According to custom, Evelyn should remain indoors and out of circulation for one month—one of the many Chinese customs associated with the birth of a daughter. But Evelyn was anxious to get home.

With Mamie's help, they convinced the midwife that she could go home on the condition that she not be seen by anyone along the way. That would be a terrible breach of Chinese custom. The solution was for Evie to be carried on a stretcher completely covered. She agreed. We were learning how to adapt ourselves to Chinese customs.

The process of moving Evelyn the two miles was no easy task. A bamboo bed, which stands about two feet off the ground, was turned upside down and lined with padded cotton quilts. Evelyn laid down and waited for the baby to be handed to her. But before she knew what was happening, the nurses covered the whole rig, securing the blanket over the upside down legs so that no one would catch a glimpse of this "unclean" woman. The baby was placed in my arms. Evelyn, her usual mischievous nature still intact, lifted a corner and peaked out at her baby and husband riding proudly in a rickshaw, while she had to submit to Chinese custom in an upsidedown bed carried by two men trotting through the streets chanting their rhythmic song.

The Bartels had moved westward to the Guizhow-Sichuan border and Rev. W.G. Davis was now our chairman. A discarded army ambulance was purchased and turned over to us for use in the villages. A little ingenuity soon turned it into a vehicle our family could travel and sleep in with comfort.

The days were getting more and more exciting. The language was coming easier now, our family had increased and we were becoming more accepted by the Chinese. Ministry was opening up to us. For several months I had struggled with Mr. Davis's decision that I would assist him as mission bookkeeper. My frustration gave rise to my first letter to the New York office begging for release from this obnoxious task. The arrival of Eleanor Morris was the answer to my prayer, and I lived for the increasing opportunities to preach in the villages.

We were the happiest people on the face of the earth, but that happiness was to be shortlived.

Even then, we could hear bombs exploding in the distance and see the refugees flowing through the city. But somehow we expected the tide to turn, permitting us to fulfill our dream of spending a lifetime in China.

10

Minnow Eyes
and Mud

EARLY ONE MORNING, FRED RUHL AND I slowly
made our way out of Wuchang in a new
two-and-a-half ton truck, which had been
purchased by the Alliance Guizhou-Sichuan Mission. Having grown up in China, Fred was fluent
in Chinese. I was about to try my linguistic wings
after 18 months of study. Our plan was to sepa-
rate, Fred driving on to his station while I would
spend the 10 days traveling on alone to Changte,
the city which would become our homebase following language school. For me, it was going to
be a sink-or-swim experience since my Chinese
was very limited. Just how limited I was soon to
discover!

After breezing through the first day, I felt encouraged. Of course, the only person I talked with
was Fred, and we only used English. The second
day was different. It had been raining incessantly,
and progress had been slower than anticipated.
With the assurance of a dry bed on the other side
of the river, we pressed on even though darkness
had already settled in. As we approached the

51

river, I could see in the headlights that the bridge consisted of only two tracks, each about a foot wide and laid over large wooden beams. It was one-way traffic only—no guard rails and only empty space between the beams.

Fred did not appear as shocked as I was, but he stopped the truck. "The floodwaters are pretty high. We'd better make sure the bridge hasn't been washed out in the middle. You walk out and see how it is out there." I was fast learning what junior missionaries were for!

I inched my way out in the headlight beams, trying desperately to be the brave junior missionary. Just beyond the range of the headlights, I discovered to my horror that a large section of the bridge was missing. I crept back and reported to Fred, who nonchalantly responded, "I thought so. They usually pull out the middle sections at flood times!"

We had had nothing to eat all day except some doughnuts Evelyn had sent along. We decided to turn around and go back to a farmhouse we had just passed and see if they would put us up for the night. I was in for some of the biggest surprises of my fledgling missionary career.

An old lady opened the door and peered out into the darkness. Discovering two "foreign devils" (a term for foreigners still in common use but without the former ugly connotation) getting out of the truck caused her to shout loudly to the people inside. A dozen or more people from the little house were soon crowded around us excitedly asking a hundred questions. Fortunately for me, Fred was there to be our spokesman.

In all of my years in China, I don't think I ever experienced more hospitable people than those simple farmers near the river in Hunan Province. When they understood that we needed a bed and food, the old grandma took charge. She ordered the men to take down a couple of doors and had them laid on wooden horses. That would be our bed for the night. I later found out that this was the typical method for accommodating guests.

Then she sent a young woman scurrying to the kitchen to prepare us some food. It was now about 9 o'clock and we were very hungry. Fred and I were seated at a table in a very dark room lit only by a tiny lamp hanging on the wall. It was too dark to see what we were eating, but it was delicious!

Since Chinese farmers go to sleep with the chickens, and it was long past bedtime, we were now ushered into our "bedroom" for the night. Privacy, however, was noticeably absent. They had never entertained such distinguished guests before and were curious to see what foreigners did when they went to bed. Watching us spread our sleeping bags out on the boards and crawl in minus only our shoes caused the biggest commotion of the night. It was not that sleeping in one's clothes was so strange, but no one had ever seen a sleeping bag before. The zippers were the most fascinating. All of the women and a few of the men had to feel the cloth and try out the zippers.

Finally, when all were satisfied, they left. We were asleep in seconds.

Breakfast came early the next morning. The young wife explained that because of the heavy rains, they had not been able to cross the river to do any shopping so she would have to feed us the same food as the night before. The delicious flavor lingering in our memories brought prompt assurances that what she had served the night before was some of the best food we had ever eaten. The cook beamed at the compliment and set about making breakfast. This time both Fred and I watched what was going into the wok to be stir fried. There were leeks, Chinese cabbage and handfuls of some mysterious ingredient from a large jar. When the steaming food was finally put before us, we discovered a bowl of minnows, complete with heads, eyes and tails! Was that really what we had eaten with such relish the night before? Remembering that we had told the young wife that it was "some of the best-tasting food we had ever eaten," we decided that if we didn't look at it, we might be able to swallow it. Besides, we didn't know when we would get another meal.

For the next two days we sat around their little charcoal fire waiting for the river to go down and the bridge to be reassembled. I learned more in those two days than in a month at school. It was very exhausting. The thought of going it alone in a few days was equally exhausting.

It looked like it would be weeks before the bridge would be restored. Finally, one man informed us that although a barge-like ferry was available for times when the bridge was out, the river was still too swift to risk a ferry crossing. That was all the encouragement we needed. Minnows were all right in the dark, but not as a steady diet for two or three days in broad daylight. Offering them twice as much ferry fare and discovering that money really does talk, we rolled the truck up onto the ferry from a steep gang plank and prepared to cross.

A strong, heavy cable stretched across the river just below the bridge. The object was to throw a line with a large hook on it around the cable to keep the barge from being swept downstream. With ugly, muddy water swirling below, our precarious position was soon obvious as the men launched the ferry by pushing away from the bank with long bamboo poles. The swift current caught the boat, sucking us downstream. The men frantically pushed on their poles to head the boat upstream toward the cable a few feet away. The man assigned the job of throwing the big hook over the cable went to work. Several futile attempts produced frantic shouting from those straining at the poles. Finally, after what seemed like an eternity, the hook grabbed the cable and everyone breathed a sigh of relief.

We made Changsha that night and the mission compound of the Bible Institute of Los Angeles (BIOLA) campus in China. From here, Fred planned to journey alone to the Province of Guizhou and I would visit Edith Alexander and the Alliance church about 25 miles away. Then I was to continue on to Changte where we expected to eventually live.

I started down the trail accompanied by a Chinese man pushing a wheelbarrow loaded with supplies for Edith. He kept complaining about how heavy the load was and suggested slyly that it was probably filled with silver dollars. His real purpose, of course, was to impress me with his hard labor so that he could demand an extra tip at our destination. Any carrier worth his weight would have done the same thing. "There are a lot of books in those trunks," I told him. What I did not tell him was that he was right—there were also silver dollars in them! Inflation was so rampant that paper money could lose half its value overnight and I had been commissioned to bring Edith about $300 in silver dollars.

Edith, a veteran of many years in China, took charge when we finally arrived. The tip she offered was less than if I had haggled with the man. Her many years of experience had honed that skill. Once we were safely barricaded inside the house, we distributed the silver dollars in all kinds of nooks and crannies she had prepared to safeguard her valuables. And then, bone-weary from the long trek over very muddy roads, I discovered to my dismay that the pastor was expecting me to speak at the church that night. In Chinese! Although my limited knowledge of the language soon became painfully apparent, I was highly complimented at the end of the service and urged to come back to speak again.

I did not know it then, but it would not be long until I would preach my last sermon in China. I'll never forget that day about a year later. Several language students went with us to the village I had been visiting. There was a strange foreboding sense in our hearts that there was not much time left. I preached with unusual power and liberty as the Holy Spirit annointed my lips. At the close of the service 13 people came forward to receive Jesus Christ as their Savior. It was probably the greatest moment of my life.

But now, I had to continue on to Changte, our future home. I was graciously received there by the pastor and given a small room with bed boards. That night, alone and with only a tiny oil lamp dimly lighting the room, a great sense of loneliness swept over me. I hadn't heard a word of English for several days and every waking moment was a constant struggle to understand and be understood. "So this is missionary life," I thought. "Where's the excitement?" The bridge and the river fit my image of exciting missionary experiences to tell people about when I returned on furlough, but loneliness in a little dark room separated from my family by hundreds of miles was not what I had anticipated.

And besides, one day my little son Jim and my newly born daughter Joy would have to go off to the mission school, and we would all experience the pangs of loneliness such as none of us could even begin to understand. I did a lot of weeping and struggling that night over the matter of surrender. As the hours passed in that little room on the hard bed, I finally said, "Yes, Lord." A great sense of peace filled my heart, and though I had many other struggles, the matter was settled once and for all. We were in China because God had called us, and we could do nothing else.

Back in Wuchang the new missionaries on the field listened eagerly to my reports of preaching and witnessing. But Paul Bartel, with his usual wisdom and insight, understood better than anyone just how significant had been the work of God in my life during those momentous 10 days.

11

One Boat—Too Many People

A UGUST, 1948 FOUND US ON TOP of Guling
Mountain, a summer resort where we
could escape the heat of the plains of
Wuchang. The year before, our summer had come
to an abrupt end when we were forced to evacuate
Rooster Mountain. As a result, everyone turned
their eyes southward to the famous mountain
town of Guling where President Chiang Kai Shek
often vacationed.

The sleepy mountaintop suddenly came alive
one afternoon as news spread rapidly that the
president would be arriving in a few hours. We
rushed down the narrow path to the village to
await his arrival. His bodyguards, their rifles and
bayonets ready for any emergency, ran before his
open sedan chair, shouting orders to clear the
path. We all pressed back against the wall and,
for one fleeting moment, looked into the eyes of
China's president as he swept by.

The following Sunday we had the unexpected
pleasure of attending church with him. Everyone
had to be seated 30 minutes before his arrival

and no one was permitted to move. The president, dressed in full military uniform and bedecked with all his medals, strode quickly and silently to his seat in the front row. It was widely reported that it was his custom to always dress in full regalia when he had a meeting with the King of kings, whether that was in public worship or very early in the morning when he prayed alone.

The routine of morning language study was followed by afternoon relaxation in the large pool or hiking along mountain trails. There were also delightful opportunities for hymnsings and good English preaching at the local Bible Conference ground. This mountain retreat provided all we needed for body, soul and spirit.

Despite the relaxed setting, an ominous cloud was hanging over our family because five-month-old Joy didn't seem to be gaining weight as she should. The missionary doctors acknowledged that she was not getting enough nourishment from nursing, but they ruled out returning to Wuchang where we could buy powdered milk. To go back to Wuchang's blistering heat, they reasoned, would be too dangerous for such a small child. But remaining here seemed foolish to us when our baby was starving.

Finally, against all advice, we decided to follow what we felt was leading from the Lord to return to Wuchang where we could purchase the much-needed food. This time, descending the mountain to the riverboat was not a problem. The sight of the steamer inching its way to the pier was an answer to Evelyn's prayer that God would have the boat at the pier instead of anchored away from shore as they often did. The captains much preferred relaying people to the ship on sampans (little flat rowboats) to docking, because they could control the crowd better. The sampan, however, created another problem—that of transferring from a bobbing boat to a swaying stairway lowered from the ship. The trick was to step from the sampan to the gangplank at exactly the right moment. We had seen many people misjudge the roll of the waves and knew that it was a fearful thing to do with little children. The filthy, muddy river never presented an exciting invitation for a summer swim!

But our hearts sank as we saw every inch of the steamer jammed with people. Canvas awnings were suspended over the open decks to provide shade from the merciless sun. Deck passage, with no conveniences whatever, was the cheapest way to travel on the riverboats. But imagine those canvas awnings sagging under the weight of hundreds of people perched precariously on top. We were confident that God would help us somehow.

We hadn't been in the Orient very long before we learned to push and shove just like everybody else. Now we were doing our share, using a suitcase as a buffer, in an attempt to reach the gangplank onto this grossly overcrowded ship. Reports of the imminent fall of Shanghai to the communists were causing many people to flee to the country. As we inched our way forward, we prayed for God to intervene and to make a way where there was no way. Within seconds, above the shouting of the crowd, we heard a voice from the ship calling loudly in Chinese, "Pastor Bollback! Pastor Bollback!" We searched the sea of faces to find the source, but with many hundreds of Chinese faces to choose from, it seemed hopeless. The caller persisted, "Pastor Bollback, Pastor Bollback, over here, over here." Finally, we saw a man frantically waving a towel out of the window of his cabin. It was Pastor Joshua Gu, the pastor of the Alliance church in Shanghai, who was now moving to Wuchang to pastor the fast-growing church there. We had met him when we first landed in Shanghai, but never expected to see him in that sea of faces. Again, God had sent His angel ahead of us.

How we ever got on the ship was another miracle. God used our white skin and long noses to pave the way! In country places when the people pointed at us and laughed, we were uncomfortable. But now, a path was being opened for us through the throngs. "Thank you, Lord, for my long nose!" I murmured. "At least it is getting us somewhere."

Safely inside and away from the press of the crowds, we sighed with relief. Pastor Gu insisted that we stay with them in their cabin. He further insisted that Evelyn sleep in his bunk while he and I would sleep in the comfortable lounge chairs in the cabin. We were getting luxury accommodations at deck space prices.

During the next few months in Wuchang a strong bond of love was forged between the Gu family and us. Their little son Sammy and Jimmy were frequent playmates, and when the time came for Evelyn and the children to leave Wuchang for the last time, it was the Gus who helped get them on the train to Hong Kong. Pastor Gu later spent 20 years in prison for His faith and for his unwavering testimony.

In Wuchang, we were able to buy the milk Joy so desperately needed, and she improved rapidly. But there was another answer to prayer which strengthened our faith and trust in a God who guides His children—there was a break in the weather. Even in Wuchang we were enjoying mountain coolness.

12

Evacuation!

WUCHANG WAS IN TURMOIL. The U.S. embassy had ordered everyone to evacuate the city on a special train that would leave in three days. Prices were escalating at an enormous rate. Fear filled every heart. Mr. Davis, the field chairman, had received permission from the Alliance officers in New York to move the women and children to Hong Kong. All the men except Mr. Davis would remain upcountry as long as possible. Everyone agreed that he should accompany the women and children since he was 67 years old and had already spent two very difficult years in a World War 2 Japanese prison camp in the Philippines.

The thought of leaving our home in Wuchang after just two years brought keen disappointment to us, but Pastor Gu urged us to go for the sake of the Chinese Christians. He knew that those associated with Americans would suffer by their presence. We expected that in a few months we would all return and everything would be back to normal again. Mrs. Ekvall, the 82-year-old pioneer missionary, assured us she had been through 11

Chinese wars and had always come back. We believed we would, too.

The day we were to board the evacuation train for Hong Kong we awakened to find that the children were not well. Jimmy was croaking with bronchitis and Joy couldn't even open one of her eyes. It was a severe case of conjunctivitus. Once again we went to the Lord in prayer to ask for direction. Should we get on that train with sick children and evacuate to some unknown place or should we try to make some advance plans for a place to stay in Hong Kong and wait until the children were better?

Following a time of prayer, we immediately sensed the peace of God in our hearts. He was directing us to postpone our departure. He also directed us to send a telegram to Hong Kong to reserve a room at the Philips House, a hotel for missionaries passing through the colony. We had never been to Hong Kong, and we knew no one there. Evelyn remembered only a place called the Philips House and, not knowing any address, I simply sent this message: "Philips House, Hong Kong: Alliance missionaries arriving Hong Kong on Friday with two children. Please reserve room for family of four."

The evacuation train pulled out minus the Bollbacks. Many of our fellow missionaries-thought we were making a serious mistake, but God had never forsaken us, and we were convinced He would not do so now. Three days later we boarded a crowded Chinese train jammed with fleeing people, but because we had made reservations the day the evacuation train left, we were able to get a compartment with just one other passenger. None of the missionaries or embassy people had such comfort and privacy on their train.

Three days later we crossed into Hong Kong about 10 o'clock at night. The blazing lights of Kowloon and the New Territories were brilliant in comparison to the dim lights of China. We had forgotton how bright the lights of a modern city could be.

As we were about to leave the train, I met an Englishman and inquired if he had ever heard of the Philips House. "No," he said, "but you can look it up in the telephone directory at the station exit." Then I asked, "Is there any place in the station where I can exchange American or Chinese dollars?" "Well, that will be a problem at this hour of the night," he said. Then, reaching into his pocket, he pulled out a Hong Kong $10 bill and said, "Here, take this. You can get a taxi out front."

As we walked out the exit, a Chinese man rushed over waving a telegram. "Are you the Bollback family from Wuchang?" he asked in English. "I'm from the Philips House. Come with me."

The Philips House was just a few blocks away on Carnarvan Road. Mrs. Philips met us and ushered us to a lovely, comfortable room. Philips House, we heard, was the registered telegraphic address for her home. Not knowing any address, we had unknowingly used the correct one. The telegram had reached Mrs. Philips even before the evacuation train arrived in Hong Kong. Most of those on that train lived for many weeks in army tents along the water front. Three days later, with Evie and the children comfortably situated at the Philips House, I headed back into China.

Parting from each other in early December was difficult because it meant we would be separated over Christmas. In fact, we didn't have any idea when we would get together again, if ever. Mr. Davis had given his son-in-law, Bob Sjoblom, and me a directive: we were to stay in China as long as we could, but leave before we got caught. That would prove to be a most difficult assignment.

Militarily, Wuchang was quiet, but Shanghai had fallen and troop movements were penetrating southward. There was no way to communicate with my family except by telegrams, which were not very satisfactory since I could send messages out but could not receive any back. Once when Al Gould, a Canadian Free Methodist missionary, and I were traveling together in Hunan, we were able to send a telegram to our wives. It said, "All safe. Don't worry. Pray for us. Hope to see you soon." In rumor-ridden Hong Kong that was interpreted to mean that we had been in some fighting zone and had been captured. Prayer meetings were held for our speedy release. We appreciated all of the prayers, but actually we were having a great time visiting and encouraging the churches.

Back in Wuchang, one of my main jobs was keeping soldiers out of Mrs. Ekvall's School for the Blind. One night, the woman in charge came rushing over to my room greatly agitated and out of breath. "The soldiers are in the courtyard," she gasped, "and they are demanding that we let them in for the night. Hurry! Come and help us." A Chinese Christian general had given us a large placard stating that his troops were not to disturb missionaries or Christians when they commandeered places to stay for the night. I quickly grabbed the sign as I ran out the door.

The courtyard next door was swarming with young Chinese soldiers already unloading their packs and demanding to enter the building. In the darkness, with everyone looking the same in their nondescript uniforms, I couldn't tell which one was the commanding officer. One thing was certain, however—I had to plant myself in the doorway and block those soldiers from entering.

The surprise arrival of a foreigner momentarily stopped them in their tracks as I strode forward in my best military style and faced them in the doorway. I held up the placard and explained to them that this was a missionary home for blind Chinese women and entry into the building was not permitted on orders from the general. We did some loud talking as they promised me that they would stay only one night and none of the girls would be molested.

One brash young fellow tried to push me aside. I stubbornly refused to budge and in a loud voice ordered him to move back. I heard an ominous click and found a rifle pointed at my chest with the young man ordering me to move out of the way or else suffer the consequences. Just then an arm reached out of the darkness and grabbed the young officer by the shoulder. A voice shouted a curt order to put the rifle down and move aside. The commanding officer had come to my rescue in the nick of time. Now at least I knew who the commanding officer was!

He assured me once more that they would stay only until morning, they would not use any of our wood for cooking and his men would not bother the girls. After conferring with the supervisor and discussing this further with the commanding officer, it was agreed that they could enter the one main room only for sleeping and that their cooking would be done in the courtyard. I passed an uneasy night, but true to the commander's word, the soldiers moved out early the next morning. Everyone rejoiced at God's intervention.

Bob Sjoblom and I had agreed that each of us was free to independently discern the Lord's leading concerning leaving Wuchang. As the ninth month of separation from our families began, it became increasingly evident that the city of Wuchang was going to fall to the communists. Pastor Gu urged us to leave. We heard from an American relief worker who came from behind enemy lines that the communists were treating the people better than the government soldiers were. Perhaps we could work with the communists after all.

It was a very difficult decision for me to make, but I finally told Bob that I was leaving. He decided to remain and guard the property. Eventually he was put under house arrest for two years, unable to have contact with the Chinese. After much discussion with the authorities over back taxes, he finally was allowed to leave. Those were hard days for me as well, remembering my dear friend was a prisoner and alone.

My suitcase had been packed and under the bed for several weeks. I shoved a few Christmas tree balls in the folds of a rolled-up crib mattress and headed for the train station. Despite the fact that the train was swarming with people, I managed to get into a boxcar and situated myself in a corner. For the next three days I sat on the mattress and slept leaning up against the sides of the train. On the third day, as we neared Canton and people began to relax a little, I suddenly remembered the Christmas balls. I had been sitting on them for three days! I was certain they had been crushed and was more than a little surprised to find they had survived perfectly. Those balls became very special to us. We enjoyed them for many years, always remembering their precarious ride out of China on an evacuation train.

Anthony and Evelyn Bollback, 1990.

Top: Anthony's parents with Jimmy.
Bottom left: Evelyn with parents, Mr. and Mrs. James Watson.
Bottom right: Mr. and Mrs. Fred Postlewaite.

Top left: Wedding day, August 14, 1943.
Top right: Arrival in Coudersport, August 1943.
Bottom left: Anthony and Dr. A.C. Snead, 1952, Japan.
Bottom right: Loading gospel tracts in Japan.

Top: Paul Bartel dedicating Judy in Kobe.
Left: September 1946, the Bollbacks leave for China.
Right: The Bollbacks' DeSoto ready to leave for San Francisco.

Top: In a Japanese hotel with Jimmy and Joy.
Right: Leaving Honolulu for Hong Kong with Jonathan and Judy.

Top: Jeep and gospel team by tent in Japan.
Bottom: Boat to Rennie's Mill for handcraft class.

Top: The house that Long Hill Chapel bought.
Left: Mr. Yang, first convert at Virtue Chapel.
Right: Handcraft assistants, Rennie's Mill.

The Bollbacks in 1965 as they left for second term in Hong Kong.

Evelyn teaching children at Shining Light rooftop school.

Handcraft products on display.

Rooftop school children lined up for morning chapel.

Evelyn with handcraft workers at Rennie's Mill.

Anthony with sixth grade graduates at Truth Primary School.

Teaching children of handcraft workers in Rennie's Mill.

Simpson Primary School, the Bollback's first rooftop chapel in Hong Kong.

View of Shining Light Primary School complex.

13

The Check

D R. A.C. SNEAD CAME TO HONG KONG to determine how to relocate the displaced China missionaries. Word spread like wildfire that all first-termers would be reassigned to another field and language with no prospects of ever going back to China. Older missionaries would be permitted to work among Chinese in another country.

This news was very disappointing to us. We had committed ourselves to China. I had also made a promise to Mr. Davis that we would reserve ourselves to return to China some day. He had said to me, "China will open again, but I will not be here when that happens. I want you to take my place and continue working among Chinese." Mr. Davis and I had become very close—like father and son. I respected him so much that I gladly made that commitment.

Our appointment for an interview with Dr. Snead was approaching. I decided to write him a letter that would reach him at his hotel room before the interview. At the appointed time, Evelyn and I walked into his room at the Peninsula Hotel in Kowloon and for the next 30 minutes we listened as he laid out plans for our lives. When he finished, I asked if he had received my letter with its request to be assigned to Chinese work to keep faith with my commitment to the Lord and to Mr. Davis. He responded that he had, but repeated that it had already been decided that we should go to Vietnam or Thailand. If we could not accept that, he noted, arrangements would be made for us to return to the States with honor. He then proceeded to briefly recount sad stories of several people who had stepped out of God's will.

My response was simple. "Dr. Snead, we fully appreciate your decision and we know you have prayed much for us, but we feel that we must reserve ourselves for Chinese work somewhere in the world. We will return to the States and wait for God to open the door." The interview ended with him praying very sincerely for us. None of the missionaries challenged our decision, but no doubt there were some who had reservations about this young couple who always seemed so certain about God's will for their lives.

It was now May 1949, and ships to the States were overloaded with fleeing refugees. We put our names on the reservation lists of several companies, but the answer was always the same: "No possibility of booking for at least six months." Although it sounded discouraging, we never waivered in our goal. We were sure we had heard from God about our future.

One day, as we again headed across the bay to check out the shipping companies, we were waiting at a bus stop on Chatham Road. Evelyn turned to me and said, "Do you have a check with you just in case we need it?"

"No," I responded a little impatiently. "We are only trying to make reservations, not buy tickets."

"You must take a check with you," she said emphatically. It was almost time for the bus to arrive and I protested vigorously while she insisted even more emphatically. Reluctantly I ran back to the apartment and grabbed the checkbook.

When we walked into the shipping office a short while later, we were shocked to hear the clerk say, "Oh, I'm so glad you're here. I have a ship going to the States via Shanghai. Two Chinese doctors just cancelled their reservations because they are afraid they will be taken off the ship in Shanghai. If you can pay for your tickets right now, you can have them!"

We walked out of that office with tickets on the *Star of Suez*, a beautiful new Egyptian ship about to embark on its maiden voyage. The news of this miracle spread rapidly among the missionaries and seemed to convince those who doubted our discernment of God's will that perhaps we had made the right decision after all.

Boarding the ship, we learned that there would be 42 passengers on this luxury freighter: 34 Protestant missionaries and six Catholic priests and two nuns. It was one of the most memorable trips we have ever taken because of the tremendous fellowship we enjoyed and the lifelong friends we made.

At Shanghai, government gunboats were trying to blockade the harbor. We made it in without incident and spent three days on-board ship with one communist soldier for every passenger. I had the opportunity to speak with one of them about the Lord and our reasons for being in China. He assured me that we would soon be able to return. I realized that many Chinese joined the communists in action but not in thought, seeking only to save their lives.

With new cargo added, the *Star of Suez* set sail after dark hoping to run the blockade. The captain seemed confident his new ship could make it through. I remember standing on the deck, watching our dream of a lifetime in China fade along with the lights of Shanghai.

Suddenly, out of the darkness of the open sea, two gunboats approached at high speed. Our captain, a burly Englishman, decided he was going to make a run for it and ordered the crew to go full speed ahead, even though the ship had never been tested that way before. As we stood on the deck, confident that we were going to make it to open water, one of the gunboats swung around and focused its powerful searchlight on us. We quickly obeyed the command to get below deck for protection. The gunboats opened fire on our ship, shots splaying across the bow as a warning to stop. Tracer bullets lit up the night sky as we huddled on the floor below deck. The captain decided to stop the ship and allow the Chinese to take off the harbor pilot. It was sad to witness his arrest.

The communist officers herded us all into the lounge and began examining our passports. Apprehension momentarily filled our hearts as they showed special interest in our China-born daughter. Fortunately, we had registered her birth at the Hankou U.S. embassy and had her included on our passport. Eventually the ship was allowed to pass into open sea.

One week out of Shanghai and still one week from California, we were standing at the railing remarking about the brilliant glow of the marine phosphorus churned up by the wake of the ship. But it was another glow we were seeing, for suddenly our thoughts were interrupted by the wail of the ship's siren and the loudspeaker blaring orders to don life preservers and report to the lifeboat stations. The ship was on fire in the middle of the Pacific!

We rushed down the already hot passageway to our cabin, grabbed the children, then ran back to the assigned station. Flames were shooting from the smoke stack, illuminating the entire deck. Even though it was a warm evening, we shivered with the prospects of aimlessly drifting on the empty sea in a lifeboat with two little children. Fortunately, the crew was able to bring the fire under control rather quickly, and we were allowed to return to our cabins. Only the blistered paint in the passageways reminded us of how differ-

ently the story might have ended. We thanked the
Lord that all had turned out well.

Early one morning, five weeks after leaving
Hong Kong, the *Star of Suez* sailed under the
beautiful Golden Gate Bridge at San Francisco.
We were safely back in the good old U.S.A. The
stars and stripes never looked so good!

Amid our joy at being safely home again, we
could not help but think of our many Chinese
friends who could not flee from the bloodbath
that was about to be unleashed on the land. How
would the church survive? Reports of suffering,
imprisonment and sometimes even death of pastors and the closing of all church doors looked
ominous. Would the church be lost forever? The
answer to that question proved to be no, for 30
years later, when the door cracked open and the
first ray of hope leaked out, the church was still
alive and well and larger and more vibrant than
ever, a testimony to the faithfulness of God and
His people.

14

Long Hill Chapel

SETTLING TEMPORARILY in Oneida, New York, in the second-floor apartment of the Watsons, Evelyn's parents, we earnestly sought the Lord for direction and a place of ministry.

One day I received a letter from Rev. L.J. Isch, district superintendent of the Northeastern District, inviting me to candidate in a little church in Chatham, New Jersey known as Long Hill Chapel. The church was about two years old and struggling. I didn't find out until three years later that the district believed the church could not survive, but had decided to give it one more chance.

The day I candidated 25 people gathered for the morning service and 15 made it back in the evening. Among those in attendance at both the morning and evening services was the Ben Jenkins family with seven children. They entertained me for the day and reviewed the brief history of the church, informing me that the church could pay $150 a month salary "plus the parsonage." I began to wonder what the parsonage must be like, for every time it was mentioned eyebrows raised involuntarily.

On the way to the church for the evening service, we whizzed past a dark road. "The parsonage is up that street," Mr. Jenkins nonchalantly
remarked, adding, "We really don't have time to
stop now, and anyway, the lights have been
turned off so you wouldn't be able to see anything." I wasn't sure what message they were trying to convey, but it wasn't a very positive one. We
learned later that the congregation was afraid we
would refuse to come if we saw the place.

Standing on the train platform waiting to return
to Oneida, I said, "Well, Lord, this is one place
I'm not coming to!" There was no response, no
rebuke, just silence. I took it to mean understanding on His part.

Three weeks passed without a word from the
superintendent. I was glad that I wouldn't have to
reject a call. At the end of the fourth week, however, a unanimous call from Chatham reached us.
The superintendent was urging us to accept. And
we did.

The people of Long Hill Chapel had a strange
fascination for the old school house where they
were holding services. It was a two-story building
with one room on each floor. It also had a highly
polished pot-bellied railroad station-type stove in
the middle of the floor and a nook for a chemical
toilet. Attendance increased so rapidly that soon
a policeman was needed to direct traffic at the
intersection on Sunday mornings. The community knew that something unusual was happening

at the old brick schoolhouse and came to investigate.

Just two weeks after we arrived in January 1950, the church held its annual meeting. With a flourish, the chairman stood to his feet and proceeded to make a speech obviously designed to impress me with the strong support of the congregation. "Since we are such a small and struggling church, pastor," he said, "we have decided we cannot really afford to give to missions during the coming year because we want to make certain that you and Evelyn are provided for to the best of our ability." His kindly face lit up with a benevolent smile as he searched for the effect his generous offer was having on me.

Stunned, I stood slowly to my feet and replied, "Mr. Chairman, and all of you good people, you have just made a magnanimous offer to us, and we deeply appreciate your thoughtfulness and love. But I must inform you that if you follow this course of action, I will have to resign tonight!" There was a murmur of dismay. The chairman's wife leaned over and spoke quickly to her husband. He jumped to his feet. "Pastor, what I stated rather awkwardly was that we want to concentrate on supporting you, and of course, we will make every effort to give to missions."

By the end of the first year, the congregation had given over $1,000 to missions while adequately supporting us. In retrospect, that was a significant confrontation which was used by God to propel Long Hill Chapel to become one of the largest contributors to The Christian and Missionary Alliance Great Commission Fund. (To the date of this writing, an aggregate total of over $6,500,000 has been contributed to missions by Long Hill Chapel.)

A corner lot across the street was donated by one of the members and plans for construction of a new building were soon underway—that is, until the church treasurer (and chairman of the annual meeting) sat me down and said, "Pastor, you really strongly emphasize faith as the key to our new building, but I'm a businessman. Only cold cash speaks. There will be no plans drawn until I have $10,000 in cash in the bank!"

God was about to teach a lesson that both the treasurer and I needed. Sunday morning I arrived for the service with a message burning in my heart and an unformed idea of how to challenge the people and break the deadlock with the treasurer.

My words poured forth that morning with enthusiasm and conviction. At the end of the message I declared with all of the conviction I could muster that I was trusting God to provide the needed $10,000 in cash by Thanksgiving Sunday, just six weeks away. With nothing in the bank and no prospects of this small congregation raising such a phenomenal amount, the people sat in stunned silence, too shocked to react. A man in the front row looked at me with bulging eyes. His face slowly flushed as it did when he was about to make an important statement. Instead of saying

anything, however, he burst into loud laughter!
The tension relieved, the congregation followed
suit while I stood there feeling very stupid and
weak-kneed.

"Now see what you've done," Satan whispered
in my ear. "You've made a fool of yourself. You're
out on a limb now for sure, and God's work will
be disgraced by your rash statement in the guise
of faith." I clutched the pulpit, looked at my people and said, "My dear friends, I don't blame you
for laughing and right now my legs are weak, but I
believe God wants a church across the street, and
I believe He will provide the $10,000 by Thanks-
giving Sunday." We softly sang the closing hymn
and went home.

About four o'clock that afternoon, one of my
strong supporters called and said simply, "Pastor,
I laughed at your announcement this morning
because I didn't believe, but God has convicted
me. I will be bringing you a check for $1,500
tonight!"

A prosperous builder called just before I left for
the evening service. "Pastor, I want to be the first
one to encourage you with a gift," he said. "I'm
bringing $1,000 to church in a few minutes!" My
excited reply was, "I'm sorry you can't be first
because I already have $1,500 promised for to-
night!" "Praise the Lord," he shouted. "It's going
to happen, pastor!"

Before the service closed, the treasurer stood up
and said, "I'm the one responsible for the demand for $10,000 in cold cash. Tonight I have

become a believer! Tonight's offering just put us over the $3,000 mark!'' Six weeks later, on Thanksgiving Sunday, the total building fund was $10,029. God had miraculously moved in and set the stage for an exciting future.

We learned many other lessons of faith in Chatham. During the winter months that first year, the prayer meeting met at our home in order to save fuel. One night at a board meeting, my dear friend and strong supporter, the treasurer, beamed as he proposed that since the offerings were steadily increasing, the church should buy a ton of coal for the parsonage since we had supplied the heat for the prayer meetings. "How do you like that, pastor?" he asked. "Can you make use of a ton of coal?" I was too choked up to answer immediately. When I could, I related that that very afternoon the coal bin had been empty, but by gathering up every piece of coal from every nook and cranny and sweeping up the small chips, I had gathered enough to have the place warm for the board meeting. There was no coal left for the next morning, but somehow I knew God would take care of us. The treasurer was not given to any great show of emotion, but that night he choked out a new recommendation, "Men, let's have two tons delivered!" When the truck pulled up the next morning, my problem was where to put two tons of coal.

15

"Off Their Hinges"

THE MIRACLE CHURCH, as Long Hill Chapel was dubbed by the district office, was a beehive of activity. As the new building began to take shape across the street, attendance continued to increase. People were squeezing into every available place. The overflow sat in the small vestibule and on the stairs leading up to the second floor. The church that had been ready to close was now the talk of both the town and the district.

The new edifice with its 250-seat sanctuary was all I had ever dreamed about: white pillars out front and a steeple from which we played a recording of church bells. The woman who had donated the property for the church also offered her beautiful new home on an adjoining lot to be used as a parsonage. But with all the joy of this growing, exciting church and the many new comforts, I struggled through every missionary conference and wrote pleading letters to headquarters asking them to allow us to return to overseas Chinese work. The response was always the same—nothing was available.

"Why can't you be satisfied here?" people asked. "We have the most amazing church in the

district, and we love you so much that you could
stay here for 25 years." I knew that, but I also
knew we were called to missionary service. Long
Hill Chapel was just a temporary detour. How and
when God would move us back to the Orient was
unknown to me, but I was certain it would be
soon.

The telephone was ringing as we returned home
one afternoon. I was surprised to hear Dr. Snead
on the other end. "Brother Bollback, we know
how much you want to be in overseas service. We
can't send you to Chinese work, but we would
like to send you to Japan. The Alliance has just
decided to reenter the country, and Mabel Francis
is pleading with us to send her missionaries with
a heart for evangelism. She says the doors are off
their hinges. Now is the time to reach Japan for
Christ. Would you consider going to Japan as
soon as possible?" I was tempted to reject the
offer, but the still small voice of the Holy Spirit
urged me to reply that we needed time to pray.
Was God sending us back to the Orient? Was this
His way of getting us back into Chinese work?
Weren't there thousands of Chinese people living
in Japan? Could this be our open door?

Evelyn and I both struggled over the invitation
to go to Japan. In the end, we agreed because we
knew there were Chinese people there. We believed that in some mysterious way God was leading us back to our beloved Chinese people.

It was a very teary board meeting when I announced our decision. One man spoke for all

when he said, "Pastor, we know you want to obey
God more than anything else. To leave this beautiful, growing church with its unlimited possibilities to go to Japan must be of God. We don't want
you to leave us, but you must obey God." Turning
to the others he said, "This is not the time to cry.
Let's dry our tears and send our pastor as our first
missionary!" And that is exactly what they did.

Although they had just topped $3,000 in the
missionary conference with the largest faith
promise in their short history, when headquarters
said it would require $6,000 to support our family
of four for one year, they promptly raised $6,000!
Suddenly, amid the tears and sorrows of parting,
they were obeying God, too. In two-and-a-half
short years, they had come a long way from not
being able to afford missions to giving to missions.

The day the new church was dedicated will forever live in our memory, because it was also the
day we were commissioned to begin work in Japan. During the Sunday school hour, we all gathered in front of the church to dedicate the Willys'
Jeep station wagon the Lord had provided. The
Sunday School members had pledged to provide
us 1,000 Gospels of John a month for street evangelism. An engineer at the nearby Bell Laboratory
proudly demonstrated a unique public address
system he had built for us and played a Japanese
record that we would use over and over again in
street meetings.

We headed to Japan assuming our transition to

another oriental culture would be easy but we soon discovered that the only similarity between the Chinese and Japanese was that both ate rice and drank tea! Some of the most traumatic experiences of our lives awaited us in the Land of the Rising Sun.

16

Where Will You Sleep Tonight?

IN RESPONSE TO MABEL FRANCIS'S PLEA to "come over and help us," we had responded with enthusiasm. However, we soon discovered that we would have to use every ounce of ingenuity to be accepted by the national church leadership. Our youthful idealism had made little allowance for the struggles we were about to experience.

During the first months, we worked diligently to find the key to the hearts of the church leaders. The only ray of hope was Pastor Tamura, a young pastor who, unlike the older pastors, was willing to accompany us anywhere for street meetings and to take advantage of our P.A. system for street preaching. We toured up and down the countryside, singing, preaching and passing out thousands of tracts and Gospels of John. He was an excellent interpreter for me, and God blessed our efforts as we traveled together.

Giving away Gospels of John by the thousands seemed like a great waste to those pastors who had suffered so many privations during the war. There was very little encouragement from anyone except Pastor Tamura. We, on the other hand, believed God had called us to spread the printed word as widely as possible. We persisted in the face of much opposition and even open ridicule. Almost 20 years later an Alliance missionary led a man to Christ who had received one of those gospels. The man described us to the missionary, sharing how we arrived in the town square and started our street meeting with the record we had been given in Chatham. He never forgot what we looked like nor the simple message I preached with the interpretation of Pastor Tamura. Most important was the little orange Gospel of John that he had cherished and read for 20 years. He explained that during those years of searching, the little book was the one ray of hope that kept him from suicide.

Although "the doors were off their hinges" and people were very responsive, we were hitting our heads against the stone wall of tradition in the local church. Frustrated by so many restrictions, we began to think about moving to the other side of the island to plant a church. Our Japanese brethren were aghast at the idea. Nobody in their right mind would choose to live on the "shadow side" of the island, where it is frequently cloudy and rainy.

In spite of the negative reaction, a young university student who was our language teacher agreed to accompany us on a scouting trip of the area. We became convinced that God was leading us to launch out and plant a church. Some said our vision was foolish and would end in failure. However, we had met a Christian family who urged us to come over and help them start a church. They promised to find us a place to rent.

Weeks went by, and as we waited and prayed, the burden grew heavier and more urgent. Almost daily the Scriptures confirmed our growing desire to plant a church in Matsue. We asked the mission executive committee to give us permission to make the move. When permission was finally granted, we were told that we would have to trust God for the funds. Nothing was budgeted for this outreach. Filled with confidence in God, we joyfully accepted this as another opportunity to trust Him. After all, not one of His promises had ever failed, and we believed He was not about to forsake us now.

Despite the news that there was still no place for us to rent, we jammed the Jeep wagon to the roof and prepared to leave. Pastor Fujika of the Fukuyama church gathered a small group of incredulous Christians to pray for us. He asked God to have mercy on us as we left our comfortable home to go to a city where there wasn't even the promise of a place to live. I could tell by his prayer that there was at best a faint glimmer of hope in his heart. We bid them farewell and headed for the mountains of central Japan.

Jimmy and Joy were filled with the excitement of this adventure. Like Abraham, I answered their questions about our new home by simply saying,

"The Lord will provide." Light-hearted and filled with the peace of obedience, we were sure that God had already prepared a place for us.

No doubt we were a strange sight as we bounced along the road singing exuberantly, "Only Believe," a song that expressed the source of our strength and lifted our spirits. As we approached the crest of the mountain, the road became progressively worse with precariously deep ruts. The inevitable happened: a sidewall punctured. We unpacked the overloaded Jeep to reach the spare tire. Soon, with repairs made and everyone and everything finally reloaded, we continued on our way with the song still ringing in our hearts.

As if to reinforce the warnings of our friends in Fukuyama, it began to rain. But, undaunted by the torrential downpour, we launched into "Showers of Blessing." We were fighting an unseen foe who wanted to discourage us, but we were unstoppable that day. It was energizing to be part of a miracle and to feel God at work.

Just 15 miles from Matsue there was the unmistakable thump of a second flat tire. The problem now was that we had no spare and it was still raining heavily. As the four of us prayed for God's help, the rain stopped. With one problem out of the way, we only had to deal with rolling the flattened tire a half mile·back down the hill to the nearest garage in Shinji.

As usual, an American stranger was a curiosity to the whole village. Who were we? Where were

we going? Why were we going to Matsue? They
wanted to know. As I talked with them, my heart
was stirred with the desire to return as soon as
possible and open a church there also. Like so
many communities in that part of Japan, there
was not one church in the entire town.

The tire repaired, we were on our way once
again. We soon pulled up to the house of our only
friend in town, an official at the local jail. Bedrag-
gled and muddy from the experiences of the day,
we just wanted to locate a bed. Silently we wondered what God had in store for us. Exhibiting
unusual excitement for Japanese, Mr. and Mrs.
Takahashi shared their miracle with us. That very
afternoon, God had provided two small rooms
which we could rent!

17

Shinji

SLEEP OVERTOOK US IN MINUTES. The rest was short-lived, however, for about midnight we were awakened by Joy's crying. Groping to find the light in the unfamiliar surroundings, we were shocked to see her covered with little red insect bites. Fleas! They were everywhere.

Early the next morning, Evelyn went to a nearby pharmacy to buy some salve to relieve the itching. At the store God had a wonderful surprise prepared for us. An attractive young Japanese woman who spoke English fluently managed the store. As Evelyn explained our problem, she produced some medication to stop the itching and then offered to rent us her home. She asked only to retain one room with a private entrance for herself. A few days later we found ourselves comfortably situated in a pleasant house on a busy thoroughfare right in the middle of town.

The flea-infested rooms were thoroughly cleaned and became the meeting place for the new church. Now, with a suitable home and a good location for the church, we plunged into the work of planting our first church on foreign soil.

Long Hill Chapel continued to provide us with 1,000 Gospels of John a month for open-air meetings throughout the region. It wasn't long before the city of Matsue knew that some foreigners had come to town.

There were only three non-Japanese families in this capitol city: a Norwegian Lutheran missionary family, an American Jewish family teaching at the university and ourselves. We had good fellowship with the missionaries, but the Jewish family was very skeptical. On our first visit to their home, the Jewish professor mentioned that he had grown up in Brooklyn, New York. With that mutual starting point, our friendship soon developed. But there was one stipulation—since he was an atheist, we were not to talk about Christianity. I assured him that the most important thing right then was his friendship. I prayed that God would open up the door for a witness in His time.

Not more than an hour after making his stipulation, he startled me by his casual remark that although he had no faith in God or religion, he often read the Old Testament. So for the next hour, we discussed the Old Testament and Jesus, the Messiah. Whenever we got together after that I could count on a long discussion about the Bible. One day, his wife called on the telephone and told us that her sister had been in a terrible accident. She asked us to pray for her sister and for them because she knew that God listened to us when we prayed.

Oguma San, a woman about our age, had come

to live with us in Fukuyama and joined us in our adventure of faith in Matsue. She was everything to us: our helper, baby sitter, cook, member of the family, inseparable friend and assistant in the work God called us to do. The church in Matsue today is the product of this lady who sacrificed and prayed with us in the difficult task we had assumed. In October of 1988, when a beautiful new building was dedicated in Matsue, Oguma San insisted that we come to take part in the dedication at her expense. Although we were unable to go, we will never forget this act of love after 30 years of separation.

During the afternoons we studied Japanese and then as soon as possible we headed out to the villages to broadcast the Good News. One day at an unmarked fork in the road, we were uncertain which way we should go. We chose the left fork. The road, which was bordered on each side by fields of ripening rice, soon was barely wide enough for the Jeep. We inched our way along and prayed that it would be wide enough to get us to the next village. Our hearts sank as the road gave way and the Jeep slid into a muddy rice paddy.

Pulled out and on our way again, we drove into a little village. Forty or 50 people poured out of the thatched homes and gathered excitedly to listen to the records and preaching. As the meeting ended, an elderly woman came and fell on her knees before us. With tears streaming down her face, she told us that she was the only Christian in the village. For 20 years she had been praying that someone would come to her town to preach the gospel.

During those first busy months at Matsue we could not get Shinji out of our minds. While the man had fixed my flat tire several months before, God had spoken to me about coming back to plant a church in that village. I made several trips to Shinji and finally was able to rent the school grounds for a week-long tent meeting. I got a movie projector from the Matsue library, and night after night we showed Moody Science films and preached a gospel sermon. It wasn't long after the tent meetings at Shinji that we were able to rent a couple of rooms, and church number two was underway.

18

The House That Chatham Built

LTHOUGH OUR RENTED HOUSE was very comfortable and daily we thanked God for providing it, we felt the need for a more permanent base. The problem, as usual, was money. There were simply no funds available for a mission residence.

We had been praying daily for God's provision of a house. Only a year earlier Long Hill Chapel had sent us out and assumed our full support. That initial step had doubled their missionary giving from $3,000 to $6,000. Now they took another step of faith and sent us $4,000 designated for a house.

One day as we searched the city for the home God had for us, we came across a very strange one nestled at the edge of town next to a great expanse of rice fields. In the distance, about 40 miles away, was beautiful snow-capped Mt. Daisen. We learned that some years before, a Japanese building contractor had visited the States and was intrigued by the American ranch-style homes. He decided to build a similar one for himself. It had been the talk of the town because it was very un-Japanese with its stucco walls and wood floors. Before it was completed, however, the builder had suffered a fatal heart attack. His widow had no desire to continue the project, and the house had stood unfinished and unused for several years.

When we realized that we could purchase, renovate and add extra bedrooms across the back for $4,000, we knew that we were special objects of a living, loving God. Our Japanese friends also understood that God was doing something unusual in Matsue. He had been preparing this house for us many years before anyone ever thought of Alliance missionaries living in Matsue.

Three years had passed since we landed in Japan, and although there was much fruit for our labors, our hearts still pulled us toward the Chinese. But how could we minister to Chinese people while living on the backside of Japan? Sometimes we felt trapped. Unfortunately our impatience showed at times. Grumbling and complaining gave way to anger and bitterness. The joy of ministry was disappearing, and we felt we were merely putting in time until furlough when we could end it all.

And then we met Bertha Cassidy. This elderly woman was the daughter of the first Alliance missionary sent out by Dr. A.B. Simpson to China. She had served many years in Japan with another mission. When we discovered that she lived near us, we made many visits to her home to sit at the feet of this honored servant of God who had passed through many deep waters. On one occasion she told us the story of her father, whom she never knew. So consumed with the desire to minister to the Chinese was he that he spent whole days in the crowded, stinking hold of a ship with Chinese laborers who were returning to China after completing their work contracts on the transcontinental railroad. An epidemic of dreaded cholera swept through the hold, claiming the lives of hundreds within a few days. William Cassidy was among them. His heartbroken young wife buried him in the international cemetery in Kobe, Japan and then returned to her native Canada. Bertha had given her life in service to God in the land where her father had died.

On one occasion we talked with Bertha about the unfairness of the Alliance policy of not permitting first-term China missionaries to move to another country to do Chinese work. It seemed impossible that the policy could ever be reversed. She responded, "Always remember that God is more interested in you than in your work. He is working in you now to prepare you to serve Him more acceptably. Be patient. Let God do His work in you." It was just what we needed to hear. We determined to obey God no matter what the cost and we told God that we would stay in Japan for the rest of our lives even if we never met another Chinese person. For the first time in three years, peace reigned in our hearts. The Chinese question was put behind us for good.

At the summer conference at the foot of famous Mt. Fuji, the Mission decided to open a home for missionary children in Kobe so that they could attend Canadian Academy, a highly acclaimed school for foreign children in Japan. We were unanimously chosen to be the houseparents. What we didn't know at that moment was that God was ready to fulfill our long-cherished dream of working once again with Chinese people. Less than two miles away from our new home was a large concentration of over 10,000 Chinese people, and in Osaka, just 30 minutes away by train, another 10,000.

Since we had just committed ourselves to Japan for the rest of our lives, we decided to let God initiate the next step with the Chinese without any assistance from us. We waited to see what He would do. And we didn't have long to wait.

The Paul Bartels were passing through Kobe on their way back to Hong Kong to take over the Alliance Press. Paul and Ina were loved by Chinese around the world and never lacked for invitations to preach. We accompanied them to one of the local Chinese congregations. God was engineering our first meeting with Chinese Christians in Japan.

The moment we walked into the church, we knew we belonged with the Chinese and that somehow God was about to work another miracle. That morning we met the McLaughlans, elderly missionaries to China who had been working in Japan since the evacuation from the China mainland. Before I knew what was happening, I had agreed to come and preach. That first assignment led to another and another and another. Our dream was coming true.

19

Hong Kong— Here We Come

W E WERE NOW BEGINNING our fifth year in Japan. A lifelong desire of Evelyn's had been to supervise a missionary children's home, and she was doing it magnificently, to the joy of all the parents. I was engrossed in the ministry at Kobe Union Church as associate pastor, and our contacts with the Chinese church steadily increased.

One night we were invited to dinner at the McLaughlans. Since they were in their 70s, they felt they must retire. However, no one in the Southern Presbyterian Mission had much concern for the flourishing Chinese work they had established.

Dr. McLaughlan struck upon the solution: the Bollbacks would take over the Presbyterian Chinese work. Their Mission had already agreed. The only requirement would be an interview with the well-known missionary doctor of China, Dr. Nelson Bell (Ruth Graham's father), who would be passing through Japan in a few weeks. With his formal approval, we could have the desire of our hearts, and the McLaughlans could retire in peace knowing that their Chinese work would continue. It sounded like the perfect plan.

With unbounded enthusiasm, we approached the Overseas Division of the Alliance for their approval. It never came. They offered, instead, to send us to Vietnam, Thailand or Indonesia to do Chinese work. Seven years had passed since we had begged to be sent to Chinese ministry. Now at last, the door was opening. Encouraged by the Bartels, we replied that we would be very happy to accept their offer if we could be assigned to Hong Kong. With our knowledge of Mandarin being revived in Kobe, we felt we could reenter ministry among the thousands of Mandarin-speaking refugees who were flooding the crown colony.

A few weeks after our interview with Dr. Bell, the Alliance appointed us to Hong Kong.

While attending our last Mission conference in Japan a few months later, a problem among the missionaries that we thought had previously been dealt with flared up again. Being determined that neither our departure nor our friendship would be marred by any unresolved disputes, we met one evening with some other couples to try to find a solution to our differences.

That night will live forever in our memories. We tried talking through the difficulty but with little success. The forgiveness we sought seemed to evade us, and so we prayed on and on, determined not to leave until all was settled. We confessed everything God revealed.

About 1 a.m. all six of us were on our knees, weeping and praying for God to meet us, when suddenly the very presence of the Lord seemed to fill the room. It was as if His hand had been placed on my shoulder as I knelt in prayer. It became exceeding heavy. I saw my awful sinfulness, and I wept bitterly. I was cleansed as I had never been cleansed before. Each one was deeply stirred until there was an outpouring of confession and brokenness from our hearts. Still on our knees, we embraced each other and wept over our stubborn willfulness. My heart was so relieved and so full of joy that I began to laugh. Soon we were all laughing as the joy of the Lord flooded our hearts.

I made one last trip to the Matsue area to conduct a tent meeting at the little town of Daito. I sensed the presence of the Lord in unusual power as I preached in that week of meetings. One night, as the invitation was given, it seemed like every hand was raised. Knowing that Japanese people responded in those days by complying with the wishes of the Americans, I repeated the invitation but made it more difficult. I asked them to walk forward to the front so that we could pray with each one individually. To the amazement of the whole team, about 200 people responded. The students from the Bible school talked for days about the mighty demonstration of God's presence and the sincerity of the people who came to confess their sin and receive Christ.

As we prepared to leave Japan, we rejoiced that the five years of intense spiritual struggle had accomplished God's purpose—we were being conformed to His image. Instead of leaving in defeat, the mountaintop meeting with God had brought us to a great climax of victory and blessing.

20

Chapels in the Sky

WITH OUR 10-MONTH FURLOUGH OVER, we prepared to sail on the *Queen Mary* out of New York to England where we would connect with the *Canton,* a passenger ship plying between England and Hong Kong.

Our anticipation grew as we approached Hong Kong after nine years of longing and waiting. The Hong Kong missionaries were at the pier to welcome us with open arms, and it wasn't long before we were immersed in preparations for one of the most exciting periods of our lives.

Thousands upon thousands of refugees had fled the crushing terror of Communist China in exchange for a tar paper shack on a crowded Hong Kong hillside. Life there was bitter, but free. As the vanguard of the younger missionaries to be assigned to Hong Kong, it seemed fitting that we be appointed to the Mission's newest ministry, the Bamboo Village rooftop chapel and school. The government had just granted the Alliance permission to construct two 20-foot square rooms on the flat top of a seven-story building that was destined to house 2,500 people in small cubicles. It was a ready-made mission field.

The complex was to be called Simpson Chapel and Primary School, which seemed fitting for such a venture of faith. Along with the assignment came the familiar information that no funds were available for the construction. Step one would be to raise $3,000 as quickly as possible so that the school could open in January. As we plunged into this new challenge with zest, God was about to work another miracle.

An article I wrote for the *Alliance Witness* (now called *Alliance Life*) evidently made a great impact because the funds began to flow to Hong Kong with breathtaking speed. The Mission was on the verge of an exciting new ministry of outreach and church planting. Simpson Chapel and Primary School became a reality. There was an air of expectancy and joy as many national church leaders gathered for the dedication of the complex and the launching of a series of evangelistic meetings. That week the first-of-its-kind core group formed and became the prototype for other new churches in the colony.

Our ministry had begun at Coudersport, Pennsylvania with 2,500 residents spread out over several miles. Here in Hong Kong, Simpson Chapel sat on top of an equal number of people all in one building. During our second term we were able to open a chapel in an even larger building housing 5,000 residents. Hong Kong was literally wall-to-wall people, and they needed Christ.

The successful beginning of Simpson Chapel caught the attention of a keen Chinese pastor by

the name of Gideon Wong. One day he came to
visit me with a startling proposition—he and I
would open a second rooftop ministry in a moun-
tainous area that was literally being leveled and
moved into the sea. Although taken aback there
had always been something about moving mountains that intrigued me and I found myself listening to this earnest young pastor. The mountain,
bulldozed into the sea, would create the Kun
Tong Housing Estate, where 26 buildings each
housing 2,500 people would one day stand. I
soon learned that Gideon's name matched his
personality. He believed like Gideon of the Old
Testament that God was able to work wonders in
response to faith.

The streets were already laid out and the building sites being prepared. We walked over the
whole area attempting to determine the best
location for "our" building. We found what we
wanted—a site near the main entrance road which
faced an area designated for a park. This would
provide unobstructed visibility to thousands of
people. By faith we stood on that spot and
claimed it for our second chapel in the sky.

At the site office we informed the housing director of our choice. He looked at us with a smile on
his face, responding that even if we were approved, sites were arbitrarily assigned by the
main office. In spite of the put-down, Gideon and
I continued to claim the site for what would later
be called Virtue Primary School and Chapel.

The letter of approval finally arrived. Gideon

and I rushed out to the manager's office where we anxiously scanned the estate map. We had been assigned to the very site we had claimed earlier.

In my youthful exuberance I expected the roof-top project would be an ongoing "approved special," thereby ensuring a continuous flow of funds from headquarters. I soon discovered there was no authorization to make a second appeal that year. While working in Japan with Mabel Francis, we had become familiar with her favorite expression when faced with a challenge: "God is in control, not headquarters!" It was not meant to be disrespectful, but rather a simple declaration of faith in the God who delights to do the impossible. With our faith buoyed by the site assignment, we prayed for another miracle—sufficient funds to complete project two.

As the building neared completion, Gideon and I walked around the edge of the roof and prayed earnestly that God would give us converts beginning with the very first meeting at Virtue Primary School and Chapel.

Families began to move into their 10-by-15-foot cubicles. Each room, with only one door and window, faced an open walkway circling the outside of the building. Luxury and convenience were not outstanding features of these spartan buildings. There was running water and bathrooms on each level, but they were communal. Even so, thousands of refugees clamored for the chance to rent these rooms, which at least provided protection from the fires that frequently swept through the squatter camps dotting the hillsides.

Gideon moved his family into one of those rooms so that he could be near the people he served. As he walked back and forth to the rooftop where work on our structure was in progress, he noticed a man in one cubicle who was always on his bunk. One day he stopped to greet him, but was given a curt reply. Some time later the Lord spoke to Gideon again and said, "Give your milk to the man on the bed." He brushed the thought aside at first, remembering that the man had made him feel unwelcome each time he greeted him. But the thought persisted and he realized God was nudging him. He went to the man's room, stepped inside his door and said, "Here is a bottle of milk for you. I hope you will feel better soon." With that, he hastily went on his way.

The next day as Gideon passed the room, the man called him. It didn't take long for Mr. Yang to introduce himself and apologize for his behavior. "I realized yesterday when you gave me the milk that I had been very unkind to you. Please forgive me." That opened the door to a long conversation, and Gideon shared the good news of Jesus and His power to heal. Mr. Yang said that for many months he had been confined to his bed. He had even been carried to this new home and was very discouraged with his helpless condition. Gideon prayed for Mr. Yang to understand the gospel message and to receive Christ into his life.

One day Gideon reported that Mr. Yang had done something he had not done for months—he had walked. Mr. Yang testified later that he had said to himself, "If this Jesus is God and alive as Pastor Wong has been telling me, and if the Bible the pastor gave me is true, then maybe He will hear me, too." Then he added, "And if God helps me walk again, then I will become a Christian."

With that motivation, he struggled to sit up on the edge of his bed and then to pull himself to his feet. Strange sensations coursed through his legs. He inched forward to a nearby table. Each struggling step brought new strength as he propelled himself to the doorway. Now he was consumed with the desire to climb the stairs to the new chapel to see Pastor Wong. Slowly and unsteadily at first, he made it to the stairs and started up from his fifth-floor room to the roof. It was an agonizing process, but the joy welling up in his heart encouraged him to go on. Finally nearing the top, he called loudly, "Pastor Wong, Pastor Wong! Look! I'm walking!"

A short while later, among the wood shavings, Pastor Wong led Mr. Yang to Christ. At the dedication of the building, Mr. Yang walked to the platform and gave a vibrant testimony of God's saving and healing power.

As we were preparing for furlough in 1964, we made a last visit to the Bamboo Village Chapel. A mother with a little girl by her side reminded us how that three years earlier we had prayed with her. At that time the woman had been holding a

two-year-old girl in her arms and requested that
I pray for her daughter who had never walked. I
assured her that I would remember to pray for her.
She looked at me with some surprise and disappointment. "Pastor, I mean right now."

The Chinese pastor had added his word of assurance, but like me, cautioned the mother that
God was sovereign and we would have to trust
Him. "You did say God can do anything when we
trust and obey Him, didn't you, pastor?" she
asked. Feeling a bit uncomfortable by the accusa-
tion in her voice, I agreed that yes, God was able.
"Then, pray for my daughter. I do believe God's
Word." Rebuked by this simple woman, the pastor and I had laid our hands on the child and
prayed earnestly for God's healing power to be
demonstrated in answer to the mother's faith. As
we finished, I wondered what we would say if she
expected to see the child walk away. I was relieved
when she simply thanked us, and still clutching
her precious child in her arms, walked away
smiling.

As far as she was concerned, God had answered
our prayer, and like the centurion who believed
Jesus and returned to his home to find his servant
healed, this mother had believed that her daughter would some day walk. Now, with her daughter
standing by her side, she was saying, "Thank
you, pastor, for praying. Jesus did heal my daughter. See, she has been walking for almost three
years!"

21

By Every Means

BECAUSE MANDARIN WAS THE LANGUAGE we had learned in China, Evelyn soon found herself taking over the women's work in Rennie's Mill as Ina Bartel retired. Mandarin-speaking Chinese from the north poured across the Hong Kong border in droves during 1949 and 1950 as the communists consolidated their hold on the mainland. Unlike the southern refugees who found it easy to assimilate into Hong Kong society because of their shared language, Cantonese, people from the north were confronted with a very different situation. They were unable to speak Cantonese and, in fact, had no desire even to try.

Reaching Rennie's Mill Camp involved a long arduous trip. Evelyn started with a bus trip, then a ferry crossing, followed by an interesting ride on a double-decker trolley through crowded, narrow streets and finally to another ferry boat for the last lap of the journey. If all connections ran smoothly, she would arrive at Rennie's Mill two hours later.

Eventually vans were introduced as public transportation to outlying areas all over the colony, and these cut travel time in half. However, the convenience was balanced by increased danger since the new road to Rennie's Mill, which consisted only of two tracks of cementlike railroad tracks, hugged the side of the mountain and had more than 100 treacherous curves. Since many of the drivers could be classified as kamikaze drivers, we finally decided to purchase our own car, which greatly expedited our work.

One of the significant means God used to minister to and through the refugees was the Refugee Handicraft Project, which was a forerunner of the present-day CAMA Services (the relief arm of The Christian and Missionary Alliance). It opened the door for Evelyn and Ina Bartel to teach these very poor and young believers lessons in honesty, excellence of workmanship, prayer for physical needs and care for one another. It was mainly through the tithes and offerings of these young believers that a beautiful church was constructed at Rennie's Mill. Through the sale of their products in a local store and in Alliance churches in the United States and Canada, many of the refugee families were able to build small cement-block houses to replace their wooden tar paper shacks. This was part of the responsibility which Evelyn assumed at Rennie's Mill as the Bartels retired from missionary service.

Christmas was always a big occasion at the Handicraft Center, and weeks of preparation went into making this a happy, joyful time for the families. One year, as we approached Christmas, we received several large barrels of used clothing from a friend in the States. We also discovered some 5-pound boxes of powdered milk in the barrels. Our whole family had been praying that God would provide special gifts for the refugee families, so when a few boxes of milk were discovered, hope rose that there would be enough for each family to be given a box. Seventeen families with young children qualified for the milk, but with Christmas fast approaching, it looked like the milk might have to be weighed out in small packages to make it go around.

"There are still several barrels we haven't opened," Evelyn reminded our daughter Joy. "Let's go down to the storage room and see if possibly there is any more milk in them." My part was to get the tightly sealed lids off the barrels. Joy's job was to reach into the huge barrels and hand out the contents to Evelyn. Can you imagine our excitement as a total of 17 boxes of milk were retrieved from the barrels? Each family would receive a prized box of milk powder. But the real miracle in it all was that this milk had been loaded in San Diego six or seven months earlier under the U.S. Navy's Operation Handclasp. The barrels had traveled all over the Pacific before reaching Hong Kong just in time for Christmas. Even before we asked, the Lord had the answer on the way right down to the exact number.

Another miracle was in the making when, through the Bartels, we made contact with a German family in Stuttgart, Germany, whose brother was a member of an Alliance church in Arizona. On the way back to the States for furlough, we took a ship to Italy. Crossing Europe by train was an exciting experience, but most thrilling was our visit to Stuttgart, the area from which my grandparents had emigrated many years before.

We have never been entertained more royally than by the Christians of Stuttgart, and we never found people more anxious to be involved in missionary work. As the result of speaking at several home gatherings and at a large state church, they began to send us $100 a month to purchase rice and other commodities for the refugee believers. They also sent us huge boxes of used postage stamps, which our son Jim processed and sent on to Colombia, South America for their stamp project. When a terrible typhoon struck Hong Kong and devastated Rennie's Mill, it was German money that provided the necessities for the believers. We found out that God works in mysterious ways to provide for His trusting children.

Soon after our arrival back on the field in 1958, I had received invitations to preach at both the Kowloon Tong and North Point churches. Since the service at North Point began at 11:30 a.m., there was enough time to preach in Chinese on the Kowloon side at an early service and then rush to the ferry to cross the harbor to North Point Church. So when Robert Patterson returned to Canada on furlough, I became the pastor of the

English section of North Point Church where Dr. Philip Teng was senior pastor.

Soon a Sunday school and children's church were added. These ministries met the needs of a great variety of people, and attendance reached 100. Many of the worshipers were overseas Chinese who had limited knowledge of their native tongue. Others hailed from Indonesia, Thailand, Burma, Canada, Nigeria, Kenya, Singapore, Vietnam, South Africa and New Zealand, as well as families of English servicemen and international students attending Hong Kong University. This was truly an international church, blending into one great family in Christ.

22

It's Tough to Say Goodbye

YOU WILL REMEMBER that during the early years of our missionary career we had struggled with the anticipated heartache of sending our children off to the mission school. For us this most difficult experience had been postponed since our children attended British schools in Hong Kong. There were so many happy years for all of us as Judy and Jonathan, our two youngest children, attended Kowloon Junior School, and Jim and Joy attended King George V High School. But all good things come to an end, and preparations were made for Jim to attend Dalat School in Vietnam for his senior year. We felt it would help to prepare him for American college life.

The day of his departure finally dawned and I realized that our family would never be quite the same again. Many friends gathered at Kai Tak Airport to bid him farewell, and buoyed up with the excitement of his first time away from home, he passed through the gate with a big smile and a vigorous wave of his hand. Mom and Dad, how-

ever, were struggling with tears and the worst ache
in our throats we had ever experienced. For Joy,
too, it was difficult as she anticipated her turn in
two years, and Judy and Jonathan wondered
aloud with dozens of questions all beginning
with "why." As the plane receded from our sight,
we stood there—a vulnerable, lonely family in a
faroff land, fearful about our son going off to war-
torn Vietnam.

The year raced by at an unbelievable pace and
before we knew it, we were standing on the pier in
North Point as Jim sailed away to college 12,000
miles away in the U.S.A. Just as we will never
forget the tearing in our hearts that day, so we will
not forget the moment our ship docked in New
York as we returned on furlough. The five of us
lined the ship's rail anxiously scanning the crowd
for that first glimpse of Jim. The flow of emotions
was like a dam breaking as one of the children
spied him in the crowd and shouted, "There he
is! There he is!" The minutes the ship required
for docking seemed like an eternity. But soon Jim
was in our arms. It felt so good. We were a family
again.

Giving up one's children to the mission school
is the greatest sacrifice a missionary must make.
Soon it was Joy's turn. Knowing that she was
extremely sensitive about leaving home, we all
did a lot of praying and preparing. We were very
grateful for a missionary family with small children passing through Hong Kong on their way
back to Vietnam. Joy assisted with the children

and this helped her make it through the gate successfully. We were all beginning to understand the cost of following Jesus. Every member of our family will carry the memory of those unforgettable and difficult partings, but knowing all the while that it is better to obey God no matter what the cost. He has His own ways of compensating and consoling His children.

23

God Isn't Finished with Me Yet

WE WERE SITTING under a lovely shade tree with Evelyn's parents on a very hot day in July 1965 when a letter arrived from Alliance headquarters. Expecting that it contained some routine information about our return to Hong Kong, I casually scanned the pages. Suddenly I exclaimed, "Listen to this! We are going to Honolulu!" Evelyn thought I was joking and had to read it for herself. There it was—an invitation to stop off at the Kapahulu Bible Church for its missionary conference. Little did we realize the long-range significance of that letter.

There was an immediate love between us and the people of the Kapahulu Bible Church. Before we boarded our plane for Hong Kong, there were a number of obvious hints that in the face of the recent resignation of their pastor they would like to have us consider the position. But our faces were set toward Hong Kong, and Hong Kong it would be.

When the plane landed at Kai Tak Airport in Hong Kong, we were met by a great crowd of friends, and after a noisy and joyous welcome, we were put up in the Fortuna Hotel in Kowloon until a decision could be made about where we would live. Finding an apartment proved to be a more difficult task than we had anticipated. No one seemed able to make any decision about how much we could spend on rent. Day after day we walked the streets searching for the right place. It was very discouraging. The invitation to remain in lovely Hawaii tempted us to write and say we could come after all since it appeared God was closing the door to us in Hong Kong. The struggle was exceedingly fierce, yet in our hearts we knew God had called us to Hong Kong.

School began for Judy and Jonathan almost as soon as we arrived, and that added additional stress to our housing problem. Living out of suitcases for weeks on end was beginning to take its toll on us all. Upset by the indecision, missing our two children back in the States and beginning to feel that it wasn't worth the trouble and heartache, our frustration almost reached the breaking point.

And then God intervened. The area secretary arrived for a two-day visit. We will never know what he did, but suddenly we were given an adequate rental allowance.

The next day I found myself walking elatedly along Prince Edward Road with my head high and my heart singing for joy. With my face lifted skyward, I noticed a rental sign on the eighth floor of a new apartment building I had passed many times during the previous weeks. Before the hour was over, we had rented a spacious apartment within the budget! That same afternoon our search for a car came to an end. It seemed like God just rolled the car right to our doorstep. That night when we gathered the children together for prayer, our hearts were bursting with praise to God. We had found an apartment and a car all in the same day! The next day we purchased some necessary furniture and moved into the eighth-floor apartment. God had suddenly caused everything to fall into place. We were home.

Then, right in the midst of our joy, a letter arrived from Kapahulu Bible Church with an official call to be their pastor. Stunned, we sat down to untangle our thoughts. How we wanted to say yes to those wonderful people who had won our hearts, but here we were, in the midst of a miracle God had performed. Three days earlier, we would have jumped at the offer, but now there was no question about what we should do. The Lord had opened the door to Hong Kong. We would continue to serve Him there.

Unexpectedly, at the Mission conference, I was elected chairman of the China/Hong Kong field. This was a traumatic experience for everyone as the Mission made its first move away from veteran missionary leadership to the younger generation. My thoughts flashed back to a day in 1949 in the city of Canton, China when I pledged to Rev. W.G. Davis, the field chairman, that I would reserve myself for China no matter what the cost.

Although the decisions that brought us to this moment had often been difficult, God had helped us to keep our hand to the plow.

As chairman I inherited the work of the Hong Kong Business Office, a purchasing agency provided for our missionaries in Southeast Asia and the Pacific Islands. It seemed impossible to add this demanding work to my full schedule of pastoring the English service at the North Point Alliance Church, supervising the rooftop chapels started during our previous term and the leadership responsibilities for 30 missionaries and 35 churches. I wrote to the area secretary and pled for a businessman to be sent out to take over the agency.

A few days later and thousands of miles away in New York, Woerner Lewald and his wife, Marianne, walked into Bill Kerr's office and made a surprising offer. Having just retired as a national buyer for the Firestone Company, they wanted to give two years as a business agent for one of the Alliance fields. Bill handed him my letter which had just arrived on his desk. In a style we all came to appreciate, Woerner replied, "When can we get started?"

What an answer to prayer! But the Lewalds' service was short-lived. In his second winter in Hong Kong, Woerner suddenly passed away. He had made a significant contribution in pioneering the concept of retired people serving overseas. Since then, retired businessmen have filled that position with great success and blessing.

The Hong Kong government was making tremendous strides in housing the refugees from China. The rooftop resettlement houses, with 2,500 people in each building, had moved many people from tar paper shacks into safe and sanitary buildings. The call of the glitter and relative peace and safety of Hong Kong reached to the farthest corners of China where misery, hunger and death stalked the land. The refugees continued to pour into the colony, creating an ever-present problem of finding housing and water. At one period we were restricted to four hours of water every fourth day because of the demand.

One day I received a visit from Pastor Tseng of the small Alliance church on Ping Chau Island. This isolated island could only be reached by a two-hour ferry ride. Pastor Tseng seemed to be the right man for this island, which lacked the simplest amenities and culture of Asia's busiest harbor. However, sitting across the desk from me, I heard him making a most absurd request.

The Hong Kong government had just opened the new development of Sao Mao Ping. They would build a five-story school for 2,000 students in the middle of a community of 16-story apartment buildings, each housing 5,000 people, and they would rent it to us for one Hong Kong dollar a month. At that time, one dollar was valued at 17 cents U.S. Like the other schools we were operating, we would be responsible to equip the building, provide the teachers and manage the school.

In return, the facility could be used as a church any time.

Now Pastor Tseng was asking if he could become the pastor of the new church. A refugee himself, he was learning Cantonese but not doing very well at it. Many people had great difficulty understanding him in whatever dialect he used. My immediate inner reaction was, "Impossible. Almost anyone but this man." Politely I tried to tell him that it would be better for him to stay on Ping Chau, but he was persistent. He repeated that he believed God was calling him to this new ministry. I had learned that when in doubt, stop and pray. I suggested that both he and I should pray about it and see what the Lord would do.

He did just what I asked him to do—he prayed. But he also did something else. He applied for one of the apartments in the new development. Yes, you guessed it. He was granted an apartment near the new school building. Since those apartments were extremely difficult to obtain, we realized that God must be trying to get our attention. The decision was made for Pastor Tseng to move.

Of all the rooftop chapels, Sao Mao Ping was the biggest challenge the Mission had undertaken. To complete the requirements of the government, God would have to provide $10,000 from a source other than the Mission budget. Taking a giant step of faith, I ordered the pulpit furniture and piano to be ready for the opening day of services. I believed God would provide the funds in time so that the spacious auditorium would accommodate a congregation of several hundred people.

One day a letter arrived telling us that a woman, formerly of Long Hill Chapel, had gone to be with the Lord. She and her husband had always been loyal supporters of the work in Hong Kong, and a memorial fund had been designated for Hong Kong. When the check arrived, there was just enough to pay for the pulpit furniture and piano. The Sao Mao Ping Chapel and School opened on time with all bills paid.

The enrollment soon climbed to the full 2,000 students, and Pastor Tseng proved to all of us that God had indeed called him to this new church. Even though his Cantonese was poor and his years on an isolated island created some problems, God knew what He was doing when He sent him to this church. This faithful man did a wonderful work for God in Sao Mao Ping.

It was the winter of 1969 and almost five years since we had left the States. There were 10,000 children and 300 teachers in the school system God had enabled us to develop through the chapels in the sky. Seven churches were firmly planted and flourishing. The church at Kun Tong where Gideon Wong served was now planning a daughter church several miles away. The Lord had one more task for me before furlough. It came unexpectedly.

One afternoon I met a friend from China days, Al Gould, who was now serving as the director for the Christian Children's Fund in Hong Kong. His organization wanted to divest itself of an orphanage for 150 teenagers near the China border. Their first choice was for the Alliance to take it over, and if we would do so, they would deed the half-million dollar property over to us without cost. This was a very appealing offer compared to the rooftop chapels, where every dollar had to be "prayed in." The facility was of the highest quality and had unlimited possibilities. Rushing back to my office, I called a special meeting of the field committee. Although they were excited about the prospects of the property, none of them wanted to take on the orphanage costs. I was given the unpleasant task of writing Al telling him we would not be able to accept his offer.

Several days passed before I could muster up enough courage to sit down and write the letter. Having signed my name at the bottom, I sat at my typewriter sadly contemplating the lost opportunity. Suddenly, God spoke to my heart and said, "Add another paragraph and say that if they want to give us the property, we will accept it and turn it into a youth camp and thus partially fulfill their desires."

I was stunned by the brashness of the thought, and I talked back to God. "I can't do that! Al made it very clear that it must continue as an orphanage." I just couldn't ask him to give us the property. "Besides, Lord," I argued, "it will make me look so foolish. I just finished saying we couldn't afford to operate an orphanage. How can we afford to run a camping program? And what would make them willing to give us the property for a camp?" The voice of the Lord was very persistent. Finally, I said, "Lord, if You want me to add that paragraph, I'll do it. But I surely don't understand what You have in mind. Al is going to think I'm crazy." It seemed that I heard God saying, "So what! Just obey Me." I sealed the envelope and dropped it in the mail box before I yielded to common sense!

A few days later I heard Al's voice on the telephone. "Our board has decided to give you the property for one U.S. dollar and allow you to use it as a youth camp. We are drawing up the papers right now." That day, Suen Douh Youth Camp was born.

Gordon Purdy, director of Camp of the Woods in Speculator, New York, was a good friend of both John Bechtel, one of our missionaries, and me. As a result of John's summer-long ministry at the camp, it was decided to finance the youth camp as part of their missionary outreach. That's how the camp came to be known as Camp of the Woods East. Each year thousands of teenagers are introduced to Christ on that wonderful piece of property dedicated to reaching the youth of Hong Kong.

In June, 1970, we left Hong Kong for the last time.

E p i l o g u e

THE 747 PAUSED MOMENTARILY at the edge of the Honolulu International Airport runway. It trembled as the pilot revved the engines in anticipation of the takeoff. As the throttle was released and the plane lunged forward, one big question filled my mind: "Oh God, what are You doing to me now?"

After six wonderful years as pastor of the Kapahulu Bible Church of The Christian and Missionary Alliance, we were ending a unique and thrilling ministry in the islands of Hawaii. When we had arrived in 1971, there was only one Alliance church in the state. Now there were seven growing, flourishing churches.

A great crowd of friends from the church had gathered to say farewell, heaping lei upon lei around our necks in an expression of aloha. In the empty seat beside Evelyn rested an unbelievable pile of concentrated fragrance.

We blinked back the tears to catch one more glimpse of Diamond Head jutting out into the emerald green Pacific. And yes, there it was—our beloved Kapahulu Bible Church, a lighthouse in the shadow of Diamond Head.

The plane veered toward the California coast some 2,400 miles away. It was symbolic of the new beginning God had ordered for our lives. As on previous occasions, we could not see the blue-print—only the finger of God pointing into the unknown. Many years before we had determined that we would follow the Lord where He led us. This day was no exception. My life's verse was pounding in my ears: "My earnest expectation and hope is that Christ might be magnified in my life, whether by life or by death. For me, to live is Christ, and to die is gain" (Philippians 1:20-21).

We had followed the Lord where He led us. We had given our lives in His service. Our only regret was that we only had one life to give to our wonderful Lord and Savior, Jesus Christ.

* * * * *

Following one-and-a-half years in Nyack and six-and-a-half years pastoring First Alliance Church in Silver Spring, Maryland, Tony serves to the present as the district superintendent of the Western District of The Christian and Missionary Alliance.

• If you were inspired by reading *To China and Back*, why not give copies to your friends? Additional copies are available from your local Christian bookstore or by calling Christian Publications toll-free **1-800-233-4443**. Use the message of *To China and Back* to touch other lives as well.

• *To China and Back* is the fourth book in a continuing collection of missionary biographies. For more information on receiving other titles in the *Jaffray Collection of Missionary Portraits,* call Christian Publications toll-free **1-800-233-4443.**

• If you would like to be put on a *Jaffray Collection of Missionary Portraits* mailing list, fill out and clip the form that follows and mail it to:

Christian Publications
3825 Hartzdale Drive
Camp Hill, PA 17011

Christian Publications will notify you when a new *Jaffray Collection* title is available.

☐ Yes! Please put my name on your *Jaffray Collection of Missionary Portraits* mailing list.

Name _____

Address _____

City _____ State _____ Zip _____

AB4